Crowned

Embracing Your Identity, Destiny and Legacy As A
Daughter of The King

ANGELA CALHOUN

Published in Dallas, TX

Printed in the United States of America

ISBN:1986041050
ISBN-13: 978-1986041058

DEDICATION

To my three princesses, Claudia, Caitlin and Morgan! You fill my days with sunshine and joy. Becoming a mother to the three of you has taught me more about love than a library full of books. Because of each of you, I see the Father in everything. You are the very reason God gave me these words. Thank you for your relentless encouragement and love.

I love you forever!

CONTENTS

Acknowledgments   i

Introduction   1

My Daughter   5

I   Birth   9

II   Life   33

III   Healing   65

IV   Forgiven   99

V   Legacy   123

A Few Truths About Daughters   143

10 Things About Being God's Daughter   145

ACKNOWLEDGMENTS

Tommy Calhoun : Your constant love and support brought back my song. Your wisdom settles my fears. It is everything to know you are always praying for me.
Tricia Collins : Thank you for your belief in me and always giving me a push when I need it most.
Jewel Thrasher : From my earliest days you never wavered, always instilling in me a deep love for Scripture.

INTRODUCTION

Daughter of the King, the little girl heart that beats inside of every woman longs to hear those words describing her. It isn't just for little girls. As adult women it fills our inmost being with an overwhelming sense of belonging. Attached to the words are the feeling of being cherished, adored, loved. Each and every person on earth has been created with a need to be chosen. Why are we drawn to stories of royalty, romance and destiny? Because we were created by the King of Kings. Our heritage in the kingdom of God is royalty. Yes, we women are daughters of The King. Embrace the title as you should. But we would be in error if we only claim the title without understanding what it means. How are we endowed with the title? What are the expectations of a daughter? What legacy are we born into and how do we pass it on?

These are just a few of the questions I began asking myself as a "daughter". It isn't enough just to make a claim. No, we fall incredibly short when we don't press into an understanding of being a daughter of God. These are the questions we will examine through this study. Today begins step one into following the call of the Father to experience His heart for you, His beloved daughter.

This is not just a Bible study and it isn't just a book. What you are holding in your hands was designed to be completely interactive. You can journey through its pages alone or as part of a group study. Either way I am here with you until you close the back cover. Together we will read scripture, answer questions and have the opportunity to worship the One who is worthy of worship. You will notice that in each section I have shared a personal story as an example of one of the characteristics God has shown this daughter. Each chapter focuses on an encounter between a daughter and Jesus. The chapters are divided into daily segments for four days. The first three days are spent diving into sections of scripture surrounding the story of each woman's life. On the fourth day I encourage you to journal your thoughts, prayers, questions, whatever is on your heart and mind. The fifth day, I believe, is the most important. On this day you are asked to set aside some time to get alone. The place and time is completely up to you. You may choose a special place in your home. Wherever you find yourself get away to a quiet place where you can listen. Yes, that's right, listen. Position yourself to listen to God. He so wants to speak to you! He has so much to teach you about being His daughter! These lessons can't be taught by me, your mom, your pastor or your best friend. The lessons can only be taught by your Heavenly Father. Now I know some of you may be saying, "But how do I hear Him?" I can't give you an absolute answer, there's no special formula for how God speaks to individuals. We are all unique and we all hear from Him differently. What I can tell you is that if you position yourself to hear from Him you will, He promised. "You will seek me and find me when you seek me with all your heart." Jeremiah 29:13 NIV and "Call to Me and I will answer you, and I will tell you great and mighty things, which you do not know." Jeremiah 33:3.

At the end of each section I have suggested a worship song. You may want to listen to this song as you read the scriptures for the day or you may want to listen at the end of your study. You might even have other music that you wish to listen to. These are only suggestions, but each song is one that I listened to as I was writing each page.

Oh, how I wish I could be sitting beside you as you read and study through this material. Although it might take us much longer because we would have to stop for coffee, cupcakes and of course dance breaks! We would sing and dance before the Lord out of pure joy! I wish I could hear all of your stories, all the stories of your childhood, your children, of your hopes and dreams. Yes, it would take us a long time to get through to the last page. God made this daughter, me, to LOVE relationships.

Can I tell you a secret? We are already friends! Even as I am typing these words I have been praying for you! I have envisioned you sitting cross-legged and barefoot in your room, because that's how I roll. With Bible in your lap, worship music filling the atmosphere, waiting for the Lord to whisper His invitation to you, "I have so much to teach you about being My daughter." My dear friend, He is so good. Take Him at the invitation. Your life will never be the same!

XOXO,

Angela

My Daughter

Do you ever have trouble sleeping? I'm a very restless sleeper. Some nights I toss and turn before falling asleep. Other times I wake up in the middle of the night only to drift back to sleep 30 minutes before my alarm goes off. Then there are the nights I wake up multiple times. Can anyone else relate to this madness? A few years ago, I was in a pretty solid pattern of sleeping well, really well!! So, you can imagine my frustration when I woke up around 2:30am. Not only did I wake up but I was wide-eyed, fully awake. Not the usual, wake up and fight to go back to sleep. I was woken up, supernaturally to be given a mission, an understanding or as some might say a Word. This was one of those times when I KNEW God wanted to talk. Please, understand, it wasn't the first time I had experienced this, but it was the most profound of any other time.

What could be so urgent that God would wake me up so vividly, so early when I was on a great pattern of sleeping so soundly? It can only be described as a revelation I desperately needed to hear even though at the time I didn't even realize it. Just two short sentences that would set me on a long and surprising journey. What was the message from God, so urgent that it couldn't wait until 7:00am....

"Angela, do you know why I gave you three girls? Because I have so much to teach you about being a daughter."

I know! You're thinking that's it? Well so was I. Questioning if I really heard that right. Many thoughts were running through my head, for example, "God I already know about being a daughter, I've been one."

In the sweetest of ways, He began to show me things never before understood about being a daughter. Things you can only see from a different perspective. Things about being HIS daughter. You see I did understand what it meant to be a daughter to my parents. I understood what it meant to have daughters. But I didn't understand what it meant to be a daughter of the Most High God from the perspective of a parent. Once I became a parent I gained a whole new understanding of the impact of God's love. When do we learn what it really means to be the daughter of God?

In true Papa fashion, He took me by the hand and led me through what some days appeared as a mine field. He knew I wasn't ready, until now. It has been a beautiful, emotional trip. I believe that is the reason you are holding this book in your hands now. You have heard Him whispering to you, "Come. Take my hand. I so want to show you what it means to be My daughter." Let us answer His call. As we journey together may we ask ourselves this question -

What is/will be our legacy as a daughter of the King?

You don't have to have a daughter, nor do you have to be a mom for God to speak to you through this journey. Oh, sweet one, my prayer is that as you find yourself on the other side of our time together you will 1) Have a deeper understanding of God's character and His love for you. 2) Be more in love with your Creator than ever before. 3) Know without a shadow of a doubt your true identity as a daughter of the King, as God's daughter!

Before you even begin I want to quiet a lie which our very real enemy, Satan may be whispering into your ears. Trust me, while many of you will never hear this particular lie, others will. The hearer may be your sister, your best friend, your mother or you! But know this, someone close to you IS hearing the smooth and deceptive tongue of the liar. What, you may ask, is this lie? It's simple and sly. He is saying "You can't trust God, you couldn't even trust your own father." "How could a father do the things or say the things he did?" "You can't trust Angela. She didn't experience the things you have." "God's love may be true for others but it doesn't apply to me." Hear this loud and clear SATAN IS A LIAR! John confirms this in chapter 7 verse 44 where he writes of Satan "there is no truth in him. Whenever he speaks a lie, he speaks from his own nature, for he is a liar and the father of lies." NASB Not only is he a liar but his objective is to rob you. Like a thief who breaks into your property to take your treasured possession, Satan wants to steal the very joy that God has put into your heart. "The thief comes only to steal and kill and destroy." John 10:10a NASB God **does** love you and He **does** want to be your Father.

There will be times when an extraordinary level of faith is required of God's daughters. To step into our calling will require scandalous faith. That may sound insane or contradictory to you now, but keep an open mind as we take a look at the definition of scandalous. It is more than you think. It is an adjective that means to cause general public outrage by a perceived offense against morality or law. Within some of the stories we will look at you can easily see how the actions of the main characters could be described as scandalous. However, these synonyms of the word are what I want you to lock onto. It is my prayer that our faith can be described to others as **outrageous** and perhaps even **shocking.** This is the type of faith we can all build a legacy upon.

Is it difficult for you to imagine God as a good Father because you have endured abuse or abandonment by your earthly father? Has it tarnished your view of a father/daughter relationship. Please stick with me. I would ask you to allow your mind the freedom to reset. Do something you may have given up on years ago. Dream! Don't allow Satan to steal the creativity that was woven into your being as you were formed in your mother's womb. Go back in your mind to the innocent little girl whose heart had not yet been broken. Dig deep to remember what it felt like to plunge forward in child-like faith. In reckless abandon you chased the longing in your heart. There you will find the place where the innocence of a daughter of the King meets the heart of her heavenly Father!

I -BIRTH

When He Calls My Name

Day One

Three? Three girls? Why was God so specific? I think the answer to that begins in January 2016. At the beginning of every new year, I pray and ask God to give me a word for the new year. This word will set the tone for the entire year. It seems like this has become a common practice for many others recently. Perhaps this is something you do as well. Usually, for me it is a characteristic or value that I ask God to develop within my life. In 2016, my word was discipline. The way that I had hoped to see this word lived out was through my spiritual life/Bible study quiet time. I asked that as I studied His word, God would show me new things about Himself. In my study, I approached the Word to learn about Him and His character. Not what He could do for me or what He would be only to me or how a certain passage spoke to my situation. I wanted to see Him, truly see Him for who He is. Is it possible that you feel the same way? You know that God has more for you than what you can see in your present situation. Maybe you feel like you have just skimmed the surface of relationship with Him. Or perhaps you are further along on your journey with God, you're far enough along to understand that there is always more! I want my life to be remembered as one constantly chasing after my Heavenly Father to know him more and more. And dear one, I want to take you by the hand to walk together on that journey. He has many rich treasures ahead of us.

Stop now to take a moment. Ask the Father to open up your heart to receive all that He has to show you. Ask Holy Spirit to unlock your ears to hear as the Father speaks tenderly to you. Trust that Jesus will rip the veil from your eyes so that you can see His plans for your life.

The Bible, it IS God's word, it is Him speaking to you! More times than I can count women have come to me and said "Angela, I just want to hear God. I don't think He speaks to me." They are so discouraged. They truly want to hear from Him. This is my response to them and my response to you if you are feeling the same, He is speaking to you. How do I know? Because He has written His words down through men chosen long ago. His word, the holy scripture, wasn't just for them, or for the first century population. It is personal and specific just for you! Just for me! How do I know this? I'm so glad you asked.

Read 2 Timothy 3:16

Every Scripture has been written by the Holy Spirit, the breath of God. It will empower you by its instruction and correction, giving you the strength to take the right direction and lead you deeper into the path of godliness.

What does this verse tell us about scripture?

_____

_____

What do you think is meant by God-breathed?

_____

_____

Seriously, can you speak without breathing? Imagine the breath of God, imagine His breath as He speaks every word over you. Imagine Him so close, whispering into your ear His words of love over you, so close that you feel His very breath on your cheek. Oh, my sweet angels, this is exactly how close your loving Heavenly Father wants to be to you every day! He loved you so much that He has given life to you, physical life and He longs to give you more, **"But I have come to _give you everything in abundance, more than you expect_—life in its fullness until you overflow!" John 10:10 TPT**

You may be thinking "but you said that His words, written long ago are for me today. How can that be?" Read Hebrews 4:12 and write it out on the lines below

_____

_____

How does this verse describe the Word of God?

_____

Now read the verse again, out loud. Yes! Out loud! Trust me, if you skip this part, you are missing a very important lesson on how God speaks. Go into the bathroom by yourself if you have to, if you don't want anyone to hear you, but just do it.

God's word is alive and when it is spoken aloud, read aloud, then God is speaking to you! His words are what you want to hear. They are life and truth and they are altogether in one place to make it easy for you and for me to connect with the One who spoke the world into being. The One who spoke my name even before my Mama and Daddy. He is the Father who spoke softly and tenderly to your heart calling you into relationship with Him. It was Him who woke me up that night and told me to write these words for me, for my girls, for you, for every daughter who longs to call Him, Daddy.

"Eyes On You" by Kristene DiMarco

We Are His Creation

Day Two

Oh, precious Lord, you are so good to us and so worthy of all our praise. You have laid out an amazing journey for my sister today! God, I pray as she dives head first in to your Holy Word that you would give her supernatural understanding of who you are! I pray that she sees Your character of love, grace, mercy and comfort. Father, allow her to feel your presence surrounding her. My mind can't conceive how I could love you more, but I know tonight I will see and tomorrow I will wonder the same. YOU ARE EVERYTHING! Amen.

If you are a mother the next words you read may transport you to another time, especially if your children are older. Or maybe you have little ones running around you now so you said these words just today, "I'm going to count to three. One…. Two…. Three" Whew, I just had a slight panic moment. Not only have I said those words, but I've had those same words spoken to me by my parents. You too? What a picture of grace and mercy the three-count can be. We or our children, probably deserved immediate discipline, but grace was given.

What is grace? It is defined as **unmerited divine assistance given humans for their regeneration or sanctification.** Well that's a mouthful just to say "a gift given to us that we didn't earn." When the three-count came, we were all probably shown much more mercy than expected. Mercy is defined as **compassion or forgiveness shown toward someone whom it is within one's power to punish or harm.** We could have been, probably should have been punished. Instead from a place of abundant love and compassion the punishment was withheld or taken over by someone else.

When the three-count came for each one of us God show us mercy by sending His Son, Jesus. He took on our debt, taking on our sin. "All have sinned and fall short of the glory of God". Romans 3:23 But then He went even further. He didn't just take on our sins, He paid the price for them. We could never do enough, earn enough, be enough to pay so great a debt. But Jesus did! "For the wages of sin is death, but the free gift of God is eternal life in Christ Jesus our Lord." Roman 6:23. Did you get that? The price for our sin was paid for us by Jesus, which, wow!! But then not only did He pay our debt, but he gives us a gift! Because of Jesus we get grace, relief from the debt we couldn't pay. As if that wasn't enough we get a gift, life eternal, in Jesus. Y'all! I can't even! When I think of what God did for me so that I can be His daughter I am overcome! What about you?

God was showing me something about Himself that I never dreamed or imagined. Those are the things I want to share with you! I am fascinated with numbers in the Bible. Once you learn to recognize a number mentioned in scripture and the significance that number carries, you can't escape the intrigue. In Scripture the number three symbolizes *the perfection of the Godhead—the Most Holy Trinity.*

The Father, God; the Son, Jesus; the Holy Spirit, the Comforter. Three in One. Perfection in the Godhead.

14

We cannot fully know God without knowing all 3. Discovering the character of all three is to know God, to love Him in fullness. To understand being a daughter we must press in to get to know God in light of each person of the Trinity. At times it may sound and seem overwhelming. Trust me, my head begins to hurt every time I try to figure out 3 in 1, they're each separate, but they are all God. Like, what?? I'm not here to cause confusion for you, just trust the Holy Scriptures.

It is always interesting how many ideas or words we attribute to scripture that are not actually in our English Bibles. We are creatures of tradition and habit. I want to debunk one of those traditions here, the word "trinity" is not specifically mentioned in the Bible. Although the idea is taught in many places. The word trinity means "three-in-oneness. There have been many who use human examples to help us as humans understand a divine concept. While no example will ever be perfect this explanation helps me and hopefully it will help you with any questions you may have. You and I live in a three-dimensional world. All physical objects have a certain height, width, and depth. One person can look like someone else, or behave like someone else, or even sound like someone else. But a person cannot actually be the same as another person. They are distinct individuals. God, however, lives without the limitations of a three-dimensional universe. He is spirit. And he is infinitely more complex than we are. That is why Jesus the Son can be different from the Father. And, yet the same. The Bible clearly speaks of: God the Son, God the Father, and God the Holy Spirit. But emphasizes that there is only ONE God. If we were to use math, it would not be, $1+1+1=3$. It would be $1 \times 1 \times 1 = 1$. God is a triune God. Thus, the term

"Tri" meaning three, and "Unity" meaning one, Tri+Unity = Trinity. It is a way of acknowledging what the Bible reveals to us about God, that God is yet three "Persons" who have the same essence of deity.

As daughters of God we want to always check the integrity of what we hear, say and share. We do this by comparing our words and actions to the Bible ensuring they line up with the only source of truth, God's word. Before you take my words as "she said it, I believe it" please open up the Word of God. Look up the scriptures below and record what each one says.

Genesis 1:26 –

Isaiah 63:10 –

Matthew 3:16-17-

John 10:29-30-

2 Corinthians 13:14 –

These are just a few specific references. One thing is true, every story, every scripture in the Bible points us to the fullness of God. We just have to be present, aware and expectant as we open up the Scriptures to read what God is speaking to us. That is why we can read any passage in the Bible and discover something more about the character and love of God. God is always more. He is longing to show us more.

All three of my daughters have similar characteristics but very different personalities. They share the same values, the same love for God and passion to live out His plan for their lives. But each one of their approach is quite different. Claudia is the first born. She is a natural leader. Of all the girls, her personality is probably the most like my husband. She's very, we like to call it, passionate. Claudia is a warrior. She loves her family and friends fiercely. Every time she tries something new, she goes after it 110%. She has a huge heart and a deep love for the Word of God. Claudia was the one as a child who wanted to try every activity. I still have the dance costumes, baton, softball equipment, flute, keyboard and pompoms to prove it. When all of our girls were young, Tommy told them "There is a great big world out there and God created a piece of it just for you. My prayer is that you go out and find yours." Claudia took his words seriously and literally. Following her graduation from college she found her piece of the world in Texas. She trusted God's calling on her life, so we loaded her up and drove her to a state and city where she didn't know anyone. With her first job and new apartment secured Texas quickly became home. I admire her independence, even if it does take her further from home than this momma would like. Peace and rest are found in knowing she is in God's plan and in His hands. Caitlin is our second born. She is so creative. Not only is she a talented musician, but also a writer. She remembers every line to every movie she has ever seen and can quote it at the drop of a hat. In her words, "God speaks to me through Disney movies." She is also creative in her thinking and the way she approaches life. We have had our share of struggles over the way she creatively cleans her room! But her heart! Oh, my goodness, her precious heart. At twenty-five years old she is one of the most mature/wise Christians I have ever known. She blows me away. Growing up I wanted her to wear lacy dresses and hair bows, she preferred jeans and t-shirts. I wanted her to play with baby dolls. She gravitated to the toy guns and holsters, bow and arrows and an explorer's backpack. Caitlin's world was outside. She was born with an adventurer/explorer's heart. God knew she would need the foundation of adventure to give her strength for the future He is calling her into. God was teaching me even then "each daughter is independent. She may not be just like you, but I gave her to you to raise her to be like Me". Today I am so thankful that He and Caitlin didn't give up on me. Then there's our baby, Morgan. She's the one who is the most like me. Not only does she look more like me than the other two, but her personality is very similar to mine. Except she has always known what she wanted to be when she grew up (I'm still working on that). Morgan is a social butterfly. She loves people, shopping and CATS! We might make fun of her obsessions with cats and kittens just a little. It's no surprise to any of us that she chose nursing as her profession. Compassion and a nurturing spirit are just a few of her qualities that will make her successful. She just wants to help others. That has never been more evident than on the three mission trips we have taken together. She chose labor and delivery because as she told me, "I can pray over the babies as they enter the world." That is her heart. With Morgan, I never had to threaten her with discipline. If she knew that she disappointed me it was worse than any restriction or "big long talk" as her sisters called them. What a lesson that teaches me. How concerned am I about disappointing God? Or do I plunge on into sin only to be corrected by discipline?

Three in one – it would take all three girls individually and collectively for God to show Himself to me. As time passed and I began listening to His voice to teach me, it was clear that He was using three specific women from the Bible to teach this lesson. There were 10 specific things about being a daughter that God wanted to show me and I believe He wants to show you as well. I share those with you at the end of the study.

Spend a few minutes writing a description of how uniquely God formed you. Include even those characteristics that aren't particularly attractive to you. As you lean deeper into the arms of God you may see them in a differently light. Perhaps this is the moment when God will show you how to break free of destructive habits. I am praying for you!!

"Behold (Then Sings My Soul) – Hillsong Worship

Squad Goals

Day Three

I have a confession to make here. I have serious F.O.M.O.! That's Fear Of Missing Out, in case you don't have a millennial in your life to interpret. In our family I am the one who is always ready to go or do whatever someone else suggests. "You're going to the grocery store? I'll go with you!" – me. "Your child is having a birthday party. Yes, I'll be there. I don't I don't have small children any longer, but I love a good birthday party." – also me. "The new restaurant is giving away free merchandise to the first 100 people on opening day? Of course, I'll stand in line beginning at 7am! It will be like party, right?" – me again! "Would you like to go to this networking event to meet new people? Absolutely!!" – you guessed it, me. It isn't necessarily a bad thing. There is something to be said for being available, informed, and open to new adventures. Only when we let that fear of missing out on something rule our lives does it become dangerous. If we jeopardize our character or integrity because we don't want to be left out then we have fallen into the trap that Satan has laid out.

What does F.O.M.O. have to do with being a daughter of the King? Thinking back on the number three we see three men accompanying Jesus at several pivotal occasions in His ministry. Jesus presented twelve men with the same invitation "Follow me". Throughout His 3 years in public ministry we follow their travels, observe Jesus perform many miracles and listen in as He speaks words of life and truth. There are times we see Jesus in situations where the only others with him were Peter, James and John. If I had been one of the twelve chosen by Jesus, I would have definitely wanted to be in this squad! For me, F.O.M.O. would have kicked into high gear. So, I wondered did these three experience the same? I seem to sense God laughing at me here. You should know God takes great delight in His children. Think about it, those of you who are moms, when was the last time you laughed at something simple, honest, or playful that your child did? Why do you think God is any different? We are created in His image, aren't we? Yes, God laughed at my innocence in asking Him, what is it about these three? Is there something You want us to learn from their relationship with Your Son? What can we glean from their relationship with You as daughters who desperately want to draw closer? In Chapter 3 we will begin to dive into the stories of the specific women God wants to use in this study. Before we do let's investigate some interesting 3's in the Bible. It seems that we see these three men quite often. Or maybe it is because we find them, only them with Jesus at very important times in his ministry. Let's take a look.

The first time we see Peter, James and John together with Jesus, apart from the others is at the home of Jairus. Next week we will look deeper into this account. Today I only want you to see the pattern that began with this encounter. "Then Jesus stopped the crowd and wouldn't let anyone go with him except **Peter**, **James**, **and John** (the brother of **James**). "Mark 5:37, emphasis mine.

These three guys have been with Jesus and the other nine from early in His ministry. They have witnessed His power, His teaching and seen Him perform miracles. My goodness, they have just come from the "other side" where he cast out a mob of demons from a man. On this day Peter, James and John will be in the VIP section to witness the events at the home of Jairus, an official of the synagogue.

The second encounter goes like this, "Six days later Jesus took **Peter**, **James**, **and John**, and led them up a high mountain to be alone. As the men watched, Jesus' appearance was transformed," Mark 9:2. The inner circle is once again privy to a deeper revelation of who Jesus truly is as they get a glimpse into his divine nature. He is the Son of God. Greater than the prophets.

Matthew 26: "He took **Peter** and Zebedee's two sons, **James and John**, **and** he became anguished and distressed." This is the third account of Jesus taking these three, separate from the others to a place of deeper intimacy. Here in the Garden of Gethsemane, knowing that He is facing the cross where he will pay the sin price for all of humanity for all time, he calls for his closest friends, brothers, confidants. Here they have the opportunity to spend the final hours with Jesus, the Savior of the world.

These men weren't just followers of Jesus. They were sons of God. In all these instances what I observe is a personal and intentional Heavenly Father. Jesus is intentionally building a relationship with these men. He is daily investing in their future, in strengthening their faith, laying a foundation that will stand up to the pressure they will face when He is no longer with them physically.

22

> "I have told you this so that you would not surrender to confusion or doubt. For you will be excommunicated from the synagogues, and a time is coming when you will be put to death by misguided ones who will presume to be doing God a great service by putting you to death. And they will do these things because they don't know anything about the Father or me. I'm telling you this now so that when their time comes you will remember that I foretold it. I didn't tell you this in the beginning because I was still with you. But now that I'm about to leave you and go back to join the One who sent me, you need to be told." John 16:1-5 TPT

What do all of these teach us about God? What are we learning about His character and His care for us?

These three men continued to spread the good news after Jesus went back to the Father. The understanding and the proclamation of Peter in Matthew 16 of who Jesus is was the statement of faith which launched what we know as the church.

> "Now when Jesus came into the district of Caesarea Philippi, He was asking His disciples, "Who do people say that the Son of Man is?' And they said, "Some say John the Baptist; and other, Elijah; but still others, Jeremiah, or one of the prophets." He said to them, "But who do you say that I am?"

Simon Peter answered, "**You are the Christ, the Son of the living God.**" And Jesus said to him, "Blessed are you, Simon Barjona, because flesh and blood did not reveal *this* to you, but My Father who is in heaven. I also say to you that you are Peter, and upon this rock I will build My church; and the gates of Hades will not overpower it. Matthew 16:13-18 NASB

Peter would go on to preach the good news of Jesus Christ for all of his life, most notably on the day of Pentecost as recorded in Acts 2. I don't know whether or not Peter struggled with a fear of missing out. What I do know is that the time Peter spent with Jesus had a radical impact on his life. I want my life to testify to the relationship I have with my Savior. The greatest commentary of life would be that every person we meet could say without a doubt, "her life provides the evidence, she is a daughter of the king."

John was also known as the disciple whom Jesus loved in John 19:26. He is found in close proximity to Jesus throughout his ministry. Like Peter John led the first century church preaching and teaching all that Jesus had done while on earth. Several books of the Bible were authored by John. One of the most impressive, to me, is the book of Revelation. Can you just imagine being the first to "see" the future, to "see" heaven before actually being there?

Of the three, we know the least about James. We do know that James was the eldest brother of John. Their father's name was Zebedee (their mother's name was

Salome.) James, his brother John, Peter and Andrew were all partners in a fishing business prior to answering the call of Jesus to follow Him.

Not much is known of his ministry after Jesus' resurrection. It is believed, however, that he lived another 14 years before his martyrdom. In fact, James was the first of the disciples to suffer martyrdom. By order of Herod Agrippa I, James was beheaded in Jerusalem in 44 AD.

The close relationship with Jesus profoundly marked the lives of these three men. During Jesus life they were front and center as He performed miracles and proclaimed truth to thousands. They were also with Him during some of the most intimate times Jesus shared with His Father. How could they continue even when Jesus wasn't with them, even when it seemed to most they were faced with the death of a dream?

Death to us can seem so final. Death apart from Jesus is final. Jesus came to bring life, not take it away. It is true, unless Jesus returns during our lifetime, we will all die physically. But what does Paul tell us in 2 Corinthians 5:6-8. If we die in Christ, if Jesus is our Forgiver, Leader, Savior, then when we die we are _____.

Three times in scripture Jesus raises someone from the dead. The first was a widow's son in Nain. Luke 7:11-16. Read these verses and answer the following.

Soon afterwards He went to a city called Nain; and His disciples were going along with Him, accompanied by a large crowd. 12 Now as He approached the gate of the city, a dead man was being carried out, the only son of his mother, and she was a widow; and a sizeable crowd from the city was with her. **13** When the Lord saw her, He felt compassion for her, and said to her, "Do not weep." **14** And He came up and touched the coffin; and the bearers came to a halt. And He said, "Young man, I say to you, arise!" **15** The dead man sat up and began to speak. And *Jesus* gave him back to his mother. **16** Fear gripped them all, and they *began* glorifying God, saying, "A great prophet has arisen among us!" and, "God has visited His people!"

How did Jesus raise the man?

_____

_____

What did the man do?

_____

_____

How did the crowd respond?

_____

_____

The second account is found in Luke 8:51-56. We will study it in greater detail in the next session. But for now, read these verses and answer the following.

> **51** When He came to the house, He did not allow anyone to enter with Him, except Peter and John and James, and the girl's father and mother. **52** Now they were all weeping and lamenting for her; but He said, "Stop weeping, for she has not died, but is asleep." **53** And they *began* laughing at Him, knowing that she had died. **54** He, however, took her by the hand and called, saying, "Child, arise!" **55** And her spirit returned, and she got up immediately; and He gave orders for *something* to be given her to eat. **56** Her parents were amazed; but He instructed them to tell no one what had happened.

How did Jesus raise the girl?

_____

_____

How did she respond?

_____

How did the crowd respond in verse 52?

_____

_____

What were Jesus instructions in verse 55?

_____

_____

     The third and final time we see Jesus raise someone from the dead is found in John 11:11-46. Look up these scriptures in your favorite version. After you read this section of scripture answer the following questions.

How did Jesus raise Lazarus?

_____

_____

What did Lazarus do?

_____

_____

What were Jesus instructions in verse 44?

_____

What was the response of those who were present at the tomb?

_____

_____

     In all three instances, there was an invitation issued by Jesus (arise or come forth), there was a response from the resurrected. The young man sat up and spoke. Jairus' daughter got up immediately and ate.

Lazarus walked out of the tomb, still bound in his burial clothes. Those were removed and he went back to his home in Bethany. We know this because we see him again in John 12.

All three times the person who is dead answers the call of the Master to be raised to new life. Second Corinthians 5:14-16 states it this way,

> **"14 For the love of Christ controls us, having concluded this, that one died for all, therefore all died; 15 and He died for all, so that they who live might no longer live for themselves, but for Him who died and rose again on their behalf.**
>
> **16 Therefore from now on we recognize no one [f]according to the flesh; even though we have known Christ [g]according to the flesh, yet now we know *Him in this way* no longer. 17 Therefore if anyone is in Christ, [h]*he is* a new creature; the old things passed away; behold, new things have come." NASB**

While I think it would have been awesome to be alive during the first century, to be one of the inner circle of Jesus followers and to witness the resurrection to life of one who was dead I'm happy to be living now. We are not missing out! If you have Jesus you have been raised to new life! You are in the "inner circle". God has chosen you as His daughter. The way we live from this point forward is how the world will know that we are part of God's royal family.

Perfection of the Godhead, the Trinity, Three in One., God the Father, God the Son, God the Holy Spirit. Jesus and only Jesus can raise us to new life. I want to allow Jesus, the Teacher, to teach me how to be a daughter of the King of Kings. Won't you join me?

"Do It Again" ~ Elevation Worship

Day Four – Journaling

"You Came (Lazarus) [Live} – Amanda Cook, Bethel Music

You did it!! You made it through one full session of leaning in, listening to the Father and stepping out on an exciting journey with Him! This is your time of conversation with the One who loves you more than all others. Use this page to journal thoughts, notes or maybe even a prayer. There are no rules and no one is going to check your answers to see if you completed this page. I can however encourage you that the more you put into any study of God's word the more He gives you back. Maybe you aren't even sure what your relationship is with God. Be honest with Him, he will bless your honesty. Have fun and know that I am praying for you as you journal.

Day Four – Journaling

II - LIFE

Daddy's Girl

Day One

My Prayer for You ~ Father, today I pray for my sister as she opens up the pages of Your Word. Surround her with Your tender love as she seeks to know you and see you! God, I pray that if her heart is hurting because of a relationship that should have been beautiful but it fell short of your design, that she might find healing in your words. Lord, I pray peace and comfort over each daughter who no longer has a relationship with her earthly father, whether by death or separation. May she see and know you today as her ultimate source. God, You are so good and I love you so much! Amen

When I was a little girl hearing someone describe me as a "daddy's girl" seemed like a badge of honor. I wore it proudly. My daddy was my hero and I knew that I was his treasure! Even as an adult, after getting married, I continued to wear it. If you are anything like me and you qualified yourself as a daddy's girl even if only when you were a little girl, then you know the sweetness of those words. Daddy's girl, it brings to mind an earthly father who looks adoringly at his little princess. For me, it conjures up memoires of sharing strawberry milkshakes, learning to ride bikes, long lazy summer days, holding onto a strong hand, learning the art of beekeeping and not being afraid. Knowing if Daddy is there nothing, I mean absolutely nothing is going to harm me. At least that's what it means to me.

Unfortunately, not every girl has such tender memories. In fact, some have sad, dark or even ugly memories of an earthly father. Please know that all those beautiful memories I described are 100% true of your Heavenly Father. He loves you so much. He would never harm you or abuse your trust. He would and did go to hell and back for you. Nothing was too drastic to secure your healing and save your life.

As you open your Bible to the gospel of Luke we meet a father who encountered Jesus. This was no chance encounter, he went seeking Jesus. Luke 8:40-42 narrates the story of the endless love and devotion of a father.

> **40** *On the other side of the lake the crowds welcomed Jesus, because they had been waiting for him.* **41** *Then a man named Jairus, a leader of the local synagogue, came and fell at Jesus' feet, pleading with him to come home with him.* **42** *His only daughter, [a] who was about twelve years old, was dying.*

Before we go forward in learning more about the daughter, we must take a closer look at her father. His name is Jairus. The meaning of Jairus is *whom God enlightens*. At the completion of this story, you will have a deeper understanding of the significance of his name.

Jairus, a prosperous man, and highly regarded by the people in his community. In reference to Jairus in verse 41 Luke uses the Greek word *archos* him which means "a ruler of the synagogue". Then in verse 49 Luke uses the Greek term *archisunagogos*, "the official who has charge of the arrangements for the synagogue services" Luke is making a specific distinction here as to exactly what position Jairus holds within the religious community. He isn't the attendant as noted by the Greek *huperetes*, from Luke 4:20. The attendant whom Jesus handed back the scrolls. The attendant does the actual work inside the synagogue. No, Jairus is the synagogue president, the leader. His duties include conducting the synagogue worship. He had the responsibility of selecting those who are to lead the prayer, read the scriptures, and teach in the service. Jairus, was a very important man. I am certain everyone in town knew who he was. What I don't know and wonder is what was the reaction of those in town who saw Jairus as he came to Jesus making his plea.

In verse 41 we are told what Jairus position was, he is

_____.

This highly respected citizen of Capernaum comes up to Jesus in the multitude of pushing and shoving individuals. They make way for him out of respect. However, he isn't there to pay his respects to Jesus. Jairus has been the one responsible for inviting Jesus to participate in the synagogue services since Jesus has taken up residence in Capernaum. But he doesn't come to greet an old friend.

For Jairus to come to Jesus for help may seem peculiar, as many times in scripture we find the synagogue leaders questioning, debating or discounting Jesus. So, for Jairus to come, publicly to Jesus was a big deal. Not only did he come to Jesus, he begged him to come to his house to heal his daughter. In fact, how does verse 41 describe his actions?

_____

With trembling hands and somber face Jairus falls to his knees before Jesus. The Greek word in Luke's and Mark's accounts is *pipto*. This Greek word means to fall down, to throw oneself to the ground as a sign of devotion, before high ranking persons or divine beings, especially when one approaches with a petition. Matthew uses the more specific word *proskuneo*. This word means to fall down and worship, prostate oneself before, do reverence to, welcome respectfully. I see his head bowed, his shoulders trembling with emotion. Here is a paradoxical scene: the well-to-do synagogue president utterly humbling himself at the feet of the simply-dressed Jesus. He has been waiting for Jesus to return, hoping he would return in time. At last He is here. Jesus is Jairus' last hope.

Remember the posture of Jairus, it won't be the last time you will see it in our study together.

On a personal note this may not seem like a big deal, but how far would you go to secure healing for your child? I can answer that question with a personal story. Each time I read this story in scripture I am reminded of the first year of my oldest daughter, Claudia's life. Even now I can picture the exact room where I was sitting. Vivid colors flood my mind, I feel the sunshine streaming through the blinds. The smells and the sounds of that Sunday afternoon in April 1992 come flooding back. Following a fun Sunday lunch with family we came home to rest before returning to church for Sunday evening services and Bible study. Tommy was in the family room, while I stretched out on the twin sized bed in Claudia's nursery. I needed a few minutes of quite to prepare for Bible study and rest my 7 ½ months pregnant body. I recognized the sounds of Tommy rustling around in the kitchen, getting an afternoon snack. Claudia had been playing in her nursery and I watched as she toddled out of the nursery toward the sound of food packages opening. Her sweet blonde curls turned the corner and out of my sight. In what seemed like 5 minutes she was back, looking up at me screaming and wiping her tongue with tiny little fists. Her wide eyes spoke a language all their own, one that no parent ever wants to see. She was in trouble and I didn't have a clue what the culprit was. I called to Tommy asking if he had given her anything to eat. One of his favorite snacks is a spoon full of peanut butter. He replied, "Only a tiny bit of peanut butter." Then I was worried, I started screaming "She's choking, get her cup!" She took one sip of juice. Lowering the cup her lips looked like a mosquito had bitten her all around her upper and lower lips. After another sip, my baby looked like she had traded lips with Angelina Jolie. It was clear then, she was having an allergic reaction to the peanut butter. We knew instantly that we had to get help. We couldn't help her. We couldn't heal her. Climbing into the backseat with Claudia, I secured her in her car seat. Tommy drove next door to my parents' house to pick up my mother. She could ride in the front seat on the trip to the emergency room. By this time only minutes had passed, Claudia's lips were completely swollen and rolled out. Her tongue was swollen out of her mouth. Tommy was driving, way too fast. I don't even want to know how far above the speed limit we were going. The only thing I knew for sure, he was not going to let anyone or anything stand in the way or stop him from reaching someone who could heal our baby girl. On the way she began choking. Mother said "Take her out of her car seat and hand her to me. If we don't clear her airway she won't make it to the hospital." Tommy was driving. Mother cleared her airway. And I cried and prayed and prayed and cried and begged God to come and heal my daughter. Come and save my daughter. And He did. We got to the hospital in record time. The doctors and nurses used the knowledge and talent God equipped them with and our baby was healed and saved. A week later, blood tests told us that she was allergic to peanut butter. Not just a little allergic. On a scale from 1-5 with 5 being the highest, Claudia was a 5. Yes, she could have died from the tiny bit of peanut butter. But she didn't because God.... I don't like to think about how we discovered her allergy. I fall to my knees before the Father every time I remember his saving power. We were willing to break the law. Let's be honest here, speeding is breaking the law. Driving with a child not buckled into a child safety seat is breaking the law as well. On that late afternoon in April, however, nothing and no one was going to stop us from securing healing for our daughter. In April 1992, much like the daughter of Mr. and Mrs. Jairus, Claudia was our only daughter. She was our "Daddy's girl'. She was our treasure.

God loves you so much! You are His precious daughter. Quiet your spirit, close your eyes and hear Him exclaim over you, "I see you there, Daddy's Girl, and I am so glad you are here!"

"Good, Good Father" – Chris Tomlin

First Born

Day Two

You have no idea how excited I am that we are together on this journey!! It may sound a little crazy for me to say, but your commitment to studying God's word is precious to me. We may not know each other well or maybe we have never met, but just knowing women are studying the word of God gets me fired up! Really it isn't strange at all because we are connected to one another through the heart of our Heavenly Father. Please know that I am praying for you as you take each step to know Him more and as you discover your position as His daughter.

As we dive a little deeper into the history of daughters and first-born children we will take a look at birth order from scripture in the Old Testament. You will gain a deeper understanding for the emphasis on family and children throughout the pages of scripture. The previous section of study required a lot of reading. Today's section is going to require reading, but also a lot of writing and recording answers to questions. There is power in writing something down on paper. Allow God to write these truths onto your heart as you record them onto paper. Are you ready? In the words of Bette Davis, "Fasten your seatbelt". It isn't necessarily going to be a bumpy ride, but it will require a lot of page turning or scrolling through scripture.

Read Luke 8:42

for he had an only daughter, about twelve years old, and she was dying. But as He went, the crowds were pressing against Him.

How old was Jairus daughter?

_____

In the Bible the number twelve symbolizes *perfection in government, or the church.*

   Luke describes a father who is desperately seeking healing for his only daughter. A daughter who is 12 years old, and just beginning to step into the young adult portion of her life and becoming a woman. In Jesus time, she was old enough to be betrothed or engaged to a man. She is old enough to start her own family, to birth children. Yet she lay dying. It wouldn't surprise us for the father to go to great lengths to bring healing to a son. In that time the son, especially the first-born son was the heir apparent to everything. He would carry on the family name, the inheritance, he was "it".

Read Genesis 27:1-40 to discover just what it meant to be the first-born son.

Who was the first-born son of Isaac and Rebekah?

_____

What was the name of their second-born son?

_____

40

Who received the blessing meant for the first born?

_____

Giving names to children in ancient times was something taken seriously. Parents didn't just choose a name because it sounded cool or different from anyone else. You might question that if you read the story of Old Testament brothers Uz and Buz. Regardless the meaning of names truly told a story about the bearer of that name. If you need convincing read Genesis 25:24-26 "When the time came for her to give birth, there were twin boys in her womb. The first to come out was red, and his whole body was like a hairy garment: so, they named him Esau. After this, his brother came out, with his hand grasping Esau's heel; so, he was named Jacob." Esau means hairy, Jacob means he grasps the heel, a Hebrew idiom for *he deceives.* Wow!

The blessing of the first born was so important to the people that Jacob would even resort to lying, deceiving and stealing. The blessing of the father was passed on to the first-born son. This is one of many stories of the blessing being passed from father to son. But what about their daughters? Just a few chapters later in Genesis we read the story of Laban, Leah and Rachel? Even though this isn't exactly a passing on of blessing, it does give a look at the priority of birth order. Laban has a situation. He has two daughters and one potential groom. Can you guess his name? Just wait!

Read Genesis 29:14-26.

Which daughter did Jacob want to marry?

_____

Which daughter did Laban give him?

_____

Of the two daughters, who was the oldest?

_____

Do you find it as interesting as I do that Jacob, the deceiver, the trickster got tricked? You just can't make this stuff up!! This is a story that could only be written by an all-knowing, all-seeing God. And though it is full of lies, deceit and scandal, it is all part of the story of broken mankind being refined by a Holy God. Teaching us, even thousands of years later a beautiful picture of the grace of a magnificent God.

Throughout the Bible as we read stories of daughters, wives, women in general we don't get the idea that women traditionally carried as much weight as a son. Take another look at Luke 8:41.

And there came a man named Jairus, and he was an official of the synagogue; and he fell at Jesus' feet, and _began_ to implore Him to come to his house;

This isn't just a daughter, one of many children. We see in scripture that this is "an only daughter" She must have been the apple of her father's eye, "Daddy's girl." I think it's safe to assume that Jairus LOVED her! And now she lies near death. She is only twelve years old. We would consider her a child; I'm sure Jairus still did. But girls were considered adults at twelve, and boys not until thirteen. She was old enough to be married, and yet she lies at the point of death. Jairus is grief-stricken.

Can you imagine the scene? We are never told what is wrong with the girl? Does she have a disease that leads to death? Was she involved in some sort of accident? We only know she is gravely ill and Jairus has gone to get help. The father's plea is recorded in Mark: "My little daughter is dying. Please come and put your hands on her so that she will be healed and live" (Mark 5:23). Jairus is on his knees "pleading" with Jesus. Please come! Please! So, Jesus goes with him.

Maybe it is a woman thing but my heart sympathizes with the girl's mother who has stayed behind with the daughter. My mind runs wild sometimes, trying to imagine what life was like in Jesus time. Today we can have answers, remedies, cures to all our questions with just a click of a button. When in doubt, Google, right? But whatever issue the girl has, Mr. and Mrs. Jairus can't fix it, but they know the One who can.

What about you? Have you been where Jairus is? Desperate? Exhausted with worry? Sick with concern? Have you sat up all night with a feverish child praying for relief? If you aren't yet married or don't have children of your own, can you remember a time when as a child your parents were this desperate for your healing? Maybe you can recall a time that isn't even related to physical illness? Have you been desperate to receive emotional or spiritual healing? Can you recall a time where your heart was breaking to the point you didn't know if you could survive?

I believe most of us can identify with Jairus. Perhaps you've been where he is, I know I have. Just for a moment let us consider his faith. He has heard the report that Jesus' boat is coming, and so he has left his daughter's side and gone down to the beach to see Jesus as soon as he lands. He isn't the only one, hundreds of others are there as well. Luke records in chapter 8 verse 40 "the people welcomed Him, for they had all been waiting for Him." No doubt, Jairus was pushing his way to the front of the line. His daughter, his treasure lay sick and dying and as a father nothing and NO ONE was going to stand in his way!

He believes that if Jesus will just touch the girl, she will be healed and live. "please come and lay Your hands on her, so that she will get well and live." Mark 5:23. Jairus is staking his faith on a touch from Jesus' hand to pull his daughter back from the brink of death.

In scripture we read that the girl's father, Jairus is a leader of the synagogue. Naturally everyone in their town would know the father and thereby know her. In this time, the synagogue was the central hub of the city. So much of life revolved around it. Because of who her father was we can assume that she is a well-known and well-loved girl. I picture her as a daughter who loved and admired her father. He must have seemed larger than life in her

How do we become a daughter? Is there anything we can do to be born a daughter into a family? No. We just are, we can only BE. Just as the daughter did nothing on her own to become a daughter, she did nothing on her own to seek healing. Because of her parent's great love for her, and the overwhelming faith of her father, Jairus made the journey to persuade the Great Physician to come heal her, now all the daughter can do, is wait.

What an incredibly accurate picture of our situation before Jesus, the Savior enters our forever. We are waiting, sick and dying. No not always a physical waiting, sickness or even death. But we are in the waiting just the same. Oh, sure on the outside we may look good. We may look like we have it all together. We may even look to others as though we have a life of prestige, something to be envied. But when I think of life without Jesus the best example I can come up with to picture the depth of how lost we are comes from Disney. Have you ever seen the Disney movie Hercules? Let me explain. According to Greek mythology, Hercules was known as a "divine hero". His father was Zeus, god of the sky and ruler of the Olympian gods. Alcmene who was mortal, was his mother. Hades the god of the underworld was determined to destroy Hercules. As the story goes, Hercules is trying to become a god and move from earth to Mt. Olympus where the other gods reside. Hades is desperate to stop him. He's made deals with many mortals in the past. When they fail to hold up their end of the bargain, Hades casts them into the river of lost souls. Though the movie is animated, the way the souls appear, floating around, blank faces, no joy, no life, no purpose, are how I envision myself before Jesus gave me life. Like sleep walking through life.

What is the quality of life that Jesus came to provide as described in John 10:10

Jesus promised us in John 10:10 "I came that they may have life and have it abundantly." That's what Jairus wants for his daughter, life, I'm just not sure he had the slightest idea of what he's about to encounter.

There is another first-born we should look at in scripture. Who is the first-born in Luke 2:7?

_____

Just as a reminder go back to Luke 1:31-35.

> **And behold, you will conceive in your womb and bear a son, and you shall name Him Jesus. ³² He will be great and will be called the Son of the Most High; and the Lord God will give Him the throne of His father David; ³³ and He will reign over the house of Jacob forever, and His kingdom will have no end." ³⁴ Mary said to the angel, "How can this be, since I am a virgin?" ³⁵ The angel answered and said to her, "The Holy Spirit will come upon you, and the power of the Most High will overshadow you; and for that reason the holy Child shall be called the Son of God.**

Jesus was called the Son of _____.

Jesus, the Son of God, God in flesh came to earth as the first-born of the new covenant God was establishing with His people. We have established that we can do nothing on our own to become a daughter to our earthly parents. But how do we become a daughter of God? Faith. Faith in Jesus. Our faith in the grace of God giving us the gift of salvation that we didn't earn, to pay a debt we could never have the ability to pay.

> **"For by grace you have been saved through faith; and that not of yourselves, it is the gift of God" Ephesians 2:8. NASB**

"And what is God's "living message"? It is the revelation of faith for salvation, which is the message that we preach. For if you publicly declare with your mouth that Jesus is Lord and believe in your heart that God raised him from the dead, you will experience salvation. The heart that believes in him receives the gift of the righteousness of God— and then the mouth gives thanks to salvation." Romans 10:9-10 TPT

We are saved from living life as spiritual orphans. Faith in Jesus the Son of God brings us into the family of God as daughters of the only true King.

Before we close today I want to revisit something from a few paragraphs back. It is this sentence "Naturally everyone in their town would know the father and thereby know her." We were talking about the daughter of Jairus, but I think God spoke this sentence as a reminder to each of us. Do the people in our lives or even the strangers we interact with at the supermarket know our Heavenly Father? Would they know we are His daughter? Are we representing Him as He truly is? I'm not throwing these questions out as judgement. They are the questions which God tenderly whispered to me about myself as I typed the paragraph earlier. Oh, Father, I want everyone I encounter to know I belong to you. As you finish this page, sit quietly before the throne of grace and allow Him to sing over you, the song of a Father!

"Awaken Love" ~ Kim Walker Smith

Giver of Life

Day Three

Before you begin today ask God to open your eyes and your heart to all that He wants to show you. May I suggest that you turn on some music and worship. If you would allow me, I might even suggest that you listen to the song "Take Courage" by Kristene DiMarco. We are going to be taking apart our focus scripture today verse by verse so I want your heart to be tender before you begin.

Read Luke 8:49

> **⁴⁹ While Jesus was still speaking to the woman, someone came from Jairus' house and told him, "There's no need to bother the Master any further. Your daughter has passed away. She's gone." TPT**

What was the news that "someone" delivered?

_____

What instruction did they give Jairus?

_____

Jairus standing near Jesus looks up to see one of his close friends pushing his way through the crowd. As he makes his way closer Jairus can feel his heart sink within his chest. The man's face is telling a grim message words cannot adequately convey. The friend must proceed with the mission which brought him to the edge of the sea, the little girl has died.

Jairus' heart is broken and he begins to weep. The next words out of the friend's mouth may not sound so strange to us: "Do not trouble the teacher anymore." The Greek word is *skullo*, which means 'weary, harass,' active 'trouble, bother, annoy someone." But I do find this a strange expression at a time like this. The "friend" who bears the bad news now advises Jairus to impose no further on Jesus.

In Hebrew the word for Teacher is **rhabbi** or Rabbi, my master, teacher, a title of respect. Jairus and every person waiting at his home were on the threshold of receiving a lesson they never anticipated from the Teacher.

Read Luke 8:50

Write the words Jesus spoke.

_____

_____

_____

Again, why had Jairus come to Jesus?

_____

_____

_____

Fear seems to be the natural response for a parent when their child is sick, diagnosed with a terminal illness or as I can only imagine, pronounced dead.

Why do we imagine that our prayers, our requests for favor and intervention, are an imposition on God? Why do we believe God has better, more important things to do? I have experienced this response from others. At times, regrettably I have felt the same way myself over the years. It is a very common belief for man. Does God really view our prayers as an imposition on his time? Does he regard the abundance of request offered up to Him as a distraction from the more important things he has to do? No! Absolutely not. And to believe this is to buy into the lies that our enemy Satan is working overtime to accomplish.

"Let us then approach the throne of grace with confidence, so that we may receive mercy and find grace to help us in our time of need." (Hebrews 4:16)

Does fear come from God? **Read 2 Timothy 1:7** to find the answer.

> **"For God has not given us a spirit of fear and timidity, but of power, love, and self-discipline."**
> **NLT**

What is given to us in place of fear?

1. _____
2. _____
3. _____

I would call that a pretty good deal. We relinquish our fear to God, trusting in Him, knowing that He never gave us fear any way.

The words that fall on Jairus ears are the most dreaded of any parent. Jesus is standing alongside Jairus when the news comes. Though Jairus knew this could be the result before his request was granted the news hits him like a ton of bricks. A sucker punch to the gut, that is what the grief of losing someone you love so very much feels like, even when the outcome is expected. But like the friend who is closer than a brother, Jesus intervenes. "Don't be afraid," he says, "just believe, and she will be healed." Do you picture Jesus wrapping his arms around Jairus to console him? Jesus feels the pain of Jairus heart. He feels our pain today. I can't imagine this scene without seeing Jesus arm reach out to this grieving father and put his hand on his shoulder. Jesus feels his pain as deeply as he felt his own at the death of Lazarus and wept salty human tears at his loss (John 11:33-35).

Rock-solid faith can sometimes falter. We hope that day won't come. We try doing everything within our power to ensure our faith is built on a solid foundation. Sometimes even the strongest among us are tempted to give up on our faith and walk away. But Jesus just won't let us go. "Just believe," he says, "and she will be healed." Just like Jairus we can lean on Him. Our fears can rest on His shoulders as He carries us past the worst that our mind can conceive.

Oh, how I wish that all the sick children of the world would be healed. And that all could be spared premature death! Regardless of the distractions along the way Jesus has set his face toward the home of Jairus. For there lies a little girl who is on the threshold of her adult life. Hold on little girl, salvation is on His way.

Jesus could have sent Jairus on ahead with a promise that the Teacher would follow. When the woman in the crowd touched Jesus, he could have told Jairus to go home and he would catch up later. When you are grieving do you want to be alone? Many times, I have told well-meaning friends that I only wanted to be alone in my grief or despair. That wasn't always true, I wanted to be comforted. There just wasn't anyone near whom I thought could bring the comfort my heart longed for so desperately. There is only One who can comfort us in any situation. He is always there, even without invitation. Jesus will never leave us alone in our grief, just as He refused to leave Jairus. Jairus comes to Jesus worried, hoping, distraught but possessing a foundation of faith. Then he encounters Jesus expecting to find one thing. But as He always does, Jesus brings more!

Read Luke 8:51-53

> **⁵¹ When they arrived at the house, Jesus wouldn't let anyone go in with him except Peter, John, James, and the little girl's father and mother. ⁵² The house was filled with people weeping and wailing, but he said, "Stop the weeping! She isn't dead; she's only asleep."**

> **⁵³ But the crowd laughed at him because they all knew she had died.**

Who did Jesus allow to go into the house with Him?

_____

_____

Word on the street was, Jairus daughter was sick and had died. Living in the south I've experienced the way friends and family love and care for their neighbors and friends when there is a death in the family. As soon as you hear the news, you gather food and make your way to the home of the person who has died. When the death is a result of the tragic loss of a young life your emotions are on overload. Our human brain can't seem to comprehend a life cut short. I have walked through times like this with friends and family. With heavy heart the tears, turn into sobs and weeping. It's difficult to hear truth though weeping and sometimes even harder to hear good news. Jesus leaves the mourners outside and takes those who have scandalous faith with Him to a place where they are about to be a witness to the miraculous power of the Son of God. Have you ever wondered why the crowd of mourners were left out and only the parents and Jesus closest disciples were allowed to enter?

Jesus had performed a miraculous healing on his way to the home. This event was very public. There were possibly hundreds of people in the area around Jesus. So why would Jesus want this to be private?

"And they *began* laughing at Him" Luke 8:52.

Can you believe it? They were laughing at the Son of God because of what He told them about the state of the young girl's life. Yes, we know the rest of the story so it is hard to imagine. Think about this for a moment though, how difficult is it for your faith to stand firm if someone is questioning you or laughing at what you are believing God for currently. I don't think excluded them for his benefit, but for the ones who are in the room. But In the crowd were mockers and mourners and unbelievers.

Matthew records when Jesus was in his hometown of Nazareth, "And he did not do many miracles there because of their lack of faith" (Matthew 13:58). Mark goes even further and says, "He COULD NOT do any miracles there, except lay his hands on a few sick people and heal them" (Mark 6:5).

Jesus removed the unbelief from the room before he ever entered the space, before he healed her.

The mourners are appalled that Jesus would say "she isn't dead but asleep". The word for sleep used here is the Greek word *katheudo* meaning *"to go to sleep," is chiefly used of natural "sleep".* As daughters we can relate to this play on words if we have truly been raised to life in Jesus. What does that mean? Before I came to the point in my life where I trusted Jesus as my forgiver and leader, before I surrendered my whole life to Him, I was dead. Of course, I wasn't physically dead. But my life had no meaning, no purpose, no direction. I was a prisoner of selfishness and frivolity. I may not have looked dead to the rest of the world. Jesus alone knew I was only asleep, not completely separated from Him but not awake to all I could be in Him. What I needed, was the same thing we all need. It was necessary for Jesus to come to my house, past the mourners, the mockers and the critics. To come straight to me, take my hand and say, *"Daughter* arise!"

While we may try to mourn privately by holding our emotions inside as we grieve the death of a loved one, the Eastern custom of mourning for the dead is anything but quiet and private. The scene in Luke 8 is the complete opposite. The mourners and wailers had begun. It was considered a duty to mourn with one's neighbor at the death of a loved one. At the home of Mr. and Mrs. Jairus the neighbors were already on the scene and fulfilling their duty. Perhaps the professional mourners had been hired already, but I think it would be too soon to have summoned them. It was hardly a faith-filled gathering." 'Stop wailing,' Jesus said. 'She is not dead but asleep.' They laughed at him, knowing that she was dead." (8:52-53NASB)

They saw the girl's stillness from man's perspective, but Jesus saw her from God's point of view, as sleep, in a temporary condition one from which she would soon awake.

Who was right about death? Was it the professional mourners? Was Jesus right? It all depends upon your perspective. It all depends upon what you are trained to see.

To the untrained eye, a painting can be good. But to the trained eye of someone who knows what to look for, it can be declared a masterpiece. I love music and have had a few piano lessons, but I can't pick out every instrument in a classical piece performed by a symphony. Listening to an aria at the opera I can appreciate the rich voices, but I can't identify each note as they are sung.

In the same way our faith must be trained, too. Peter, James, and John as well as Mr. and Mrs. Jairus were invited into the room for training. Training to have faith beyond the obvious. Faith to hear the voice of the Father state what his will is in the situation. Faith to speak the word of faith that brings God's will into reality. Jesus desires our faith to execute on earth the will of the Father.

Then there is the laughter of unbelief in the room. There will always be the realists, the scoffers who scorn believing only in the known rules of this realm. Their belief in only what they can see keep them locked in the infant stage when it comes to spiritual realities. "They laughed at him, knowing that she was dead" (8:53). But what did they know in the face of God? Jairus and his wife had the wisdom and self-discipline to cling to Jesus' words of faith rather than the mockers' words of scorn.

"But he took her by the hand and said, 'My child, get up!' Her spirit returned, and at once she stood up." (8:54-55)

Can you picture it? The chaos and unbelief of the household has been closed out. Jesus kneels by the girl's bed. He takes her hand in his and speaks a gentle sound into her unhearing ears: "Child, arise!"

Mark, in his version of this story quotes the Aramaic Jesus would have spoken to her. Walking into the room Jesus called to her, "Talitha cumi. "Little girl, I say to you, arise" (Mark 5:41). In Luke's account Jesus calls her "child." The Greek word for "child" or "girl" is *pais*, "child". The word isn't specific for age. But Jesus addresses her directly as "Child." The second word he says is "Get up!" It is the Greek word *egeiro*, which means "to wake up, stir oneself, rise up, rise from the dead."

With all eyes on the daughter of Jairus, Luke records, "Her spirit returned, and at once she stood up." She didn't have to lie there for hours or even minutes for the energy to gradually enter her body until she could raise her head and then her body. The Greek word is *parachrema*, "at once, immediately." This was an instant resurrection!

What are the next words from Jesus mouth? Record them below as you let the thought sink in.

Luke 8:55:

_____

_____

I am so intrigued by Jesus' calmness in the midst of this incredible miracle. We don't know how long she has been sick. How often do you feel like eating when you are sick? What is the one thing you want as soon as you feel better? If you are anything like me, physically, I want food! Jesus reminds the parents that she is hungry and needs some food. Why do you think Luke would record this? He may have recorded this detail for a couple of reasons. It is possible that he recorded it to indicate that she is well, evidenced by the fact that her hunger is restored. But the most likely reason could be to indicate that she has been raised as a flesh-and-blood person, not a spirit that would not require food (see Luke 24:41-43).

What were the instructions given to the parents by Jesus? Record the words of Jesus from verse 56.

_____

_____

_____

_____

What on earth?? Jesus told them not to tell anyone what just happened. Imagine the response from Mrs. Jairus, "You've just raised my baby girl from the dead and you don't want me to tell anyone? What about all those people outside? What are we supposed to tell them? They knew she was dead. And besides, have you noticed, I'm a woman, I mean we do love to talk and share good news." At least that's what I imagine my response would have been. Why did Jesus say this? One explanation is that the more word spread of his astounding miracles, the more he would be mobbed, and the less easily he could move about. After the healing of a leper, Mark records:

"Jesus sent him away at once with a strong warning: 'See that you don't tell this to anyone....' Instead he went out and began to talk freely, spreading the news. As a result, Jesus could no longer enter a town openly but stayed outside in lonely places. Yet the people still came to him from everywhere." (Mark 1:43-45)

Another reason is Jesus' reluctance to be hailed prematurely as the Messiah. That would cut his ministry short, since it would accelerate plots against his life. In fact, he was arrested and tried for just such a concern on the part of the religious establishment (Luke 22:67)

However, I wonder how the parents were able to keep silent about the girl's resurrection. Still the word spread, but the parents were clearly told not to tell the details of what happened. Because we have the story recorded in the Gospels of Matthew, Mark and Luke we do know someone who told -- the disciples. And aren't we glad they did. What a building block to our faith! We have a recording of what scandalous faith looks like, the kind of faith I want for myself. Do you feel the same? Take a moment for self-evaluation, this is not a judgement call, merely where are the areas you would present before the Lord and ask Him to help your unbelief?

I have had the incredible opportunity to be part of mission trips to other countries. The faith of the beautiful people in these countries looks differently from that of most of us in western culture. There are many speculations as to why this is, but the truth is they just BELIEVE! Before departing the U.S. each time, I have prayed and asked God to increase my faith. God always delivers. There is one incident that stands out to me above the others. It occurred on my first trip to Africa. I had prayed and asked God to allow me to see Him raise someone from the dead. Well of course I had it all figured out how that would happen. To the depths of my soul I believed that I would see a miracle, the very one I asked to see. On this particular trip we were helping with wellness checks in various villages. There was one day when the nurse leading our team asked a few ladies to go visit a hospital in the area. Out of the larger group who went into the children's ward a couple of us were asked to go visit one specific girl. Throughout my life I have spent more than my share of time in hospitals. As a child my mother was in and out of the hospital more times than I care to remember. Heart disease ruled our days and nights and marked my young mind in a way that I prayed my daughters would never experience. Suffice it to say I have seen every type of patient room, recovery area packed with patients and waiting room you can imagine. I have seen multiple tubes leading from every part of a human body. The gray flesh of a person fresh from open heart surgery has been enough to make the strongest men in my family faint. None of those could come close to preparing me for what I would witness on that day in Africa when God would answer my prayer in His way.

Upon entering this specific area of the hospital our eyes fell upon rows and rows of beds filling one large room. No walls, no curtains separated the patients. There was no privacy afforded to those who found themselves in this section. Pain, suffering and shame were on display for all who crossed the room to visit with the patients. Making our way through the area we could not help but to notice so many people, with various ailments, each watching as the pale skinned women walked past. The journey ended beside the bed of a 15-year-old girl. Her slim frame lay motionless on the stark white sheets, her eyes, although open, showed no emotion. Our leader Jenny moved closer and spoke the young girl's name. Sitting up in her bed with eyes avoiding ours, Jenny began speaking directly to her with a soothing voice of love and compassion. The reason this beautiful girl was in the hospital was horrendous to all who stood surrounding her bed. Days earlier this precious "child" had tried to take her own life by swallowing rat poison. Someone so young with so much life yet to be lived, what could possibly drive her to these drastic measures. A family member had sexually assaulted her. The person this girl should have been able to trust had done the unthinkable, he had raped her. I only imagine the voices that mocked her with lies of shame, fear and hate. She never told us and we didn't ask for the specifics of what led her to her actions. I'm not sure she could have vocalized them if she wanted to. Poisoning is drastic and the antidote for such almost unbearable. What this sweet girl had yet to perceive was that surrounding her bed were sisters whose hearts ached for the drama of our plight. Around her bed stood women who themselves had been raped, sexually abused, neglected and survived suicide attempts. Even Jenny could not have known the past secrets of the daughters of God who accompanied her on that warm May afternoon. We didn't linger in her room all day. The women did most of the talking because the throat of the young girl was still sore and her voice weak and raspy. The words spoken over her were all straight from the heart of God. Later in the day most of us couldn't even remember what we did say and the words we had prepared in advance from our own hearts were never uttered in the room. God spoke words of life to the girl. He spoke them through our mouths, He used our tongues that day. Even as we spoke frail arms stayed by her side, her head bowed, eyes barely lifting to look at the women. When she did look up her eyes were haunting, lifeless, hopeless. One of the ladies laid a Bible in her lap and spoke words that even today I can't recall, they were holy, from the Lord. The lifeless eyes fell upon the cover. And then it happened!! She looked up at all of us, met each of us eye-to-eye. Gone were the haunting eyes of one who has no hope. Her face radiated with life. Her smile, yes, I said her SMILE, proclaimed hope and faith in the One who brings joy. It was the first time we had seen any expression on her face at all! Jesus had raised this beautiful daughter to LIFE before our very eyes! I still can't type these words without tears flowing from my eyes, eyes that will never forget the day I witnessed a miracle.

I thought I had it all figured out how God would raise someone from the dead. Honestly, I thought we would walk into a mud hut where a grandfather or a child lay lifeless, the breath leaving his lungs. Then the creator of heaven and earth, the giver of life would breathe the *ruach* into the limp body. *Ruach* means breath, wind, spirit. I have given you the full definition I found on the Bible Hub website so you can grasp the fullness of this word that goes far beyond what we imagine as the air in the human lungs. The original Hebrew Word: ר‎וּחַ is a feminine noun with the transliteration of *ruach*. The short definition of ruach is spirit. It is also defined as breath, wind, spirit. This is one of my favorite Hebrew words. So naturally I spent a lot of time researching the meaning and uses of the word throughout the Bible. In the NASB it is also translated as air, anger, blast, breath into the body. Even to this day I can say, I am so glad God chose to answer my prayer in the way He did. My faith grew exponentially that day! I think not only mine, but everyone else surrounding that tiny bed. God is so much greater than what we give Him credit for, He knows us better than we can imagine. He knows what we need and when we need it because He wove us together beautifully.

That experience is still so tender and real to me. I want to shout it to the mountain tops. But I don't run out my front door telling everyone I meet. Why? Because that isn't what God has told me to do. Not everyone I meet is ready to hear. For this very reason it is imperative that we stay in tune with God. We must be consistently listening for His voice to discern if we are following His will and not our own. The New Living Translation ends the story with these words, "Her parents were overwhelmed, but Jesus insisted that they not tell anyone what had happened." Vs. 56.

Seriously, don't tell anyone? Why? That's a good question, but one that isn't answered. Even if they didn't tell anyone else, can't you imagine they talked about it among themselves. I certainly would. And I think Jairus and Mrs. Jairus made sure their children, their children's children and generation after generation knew exactly who the true Giver of Life was.

How can we as daughters live a life of faith in our Father? Can we together pledge to teach our children and their children that faith in Jesus at all times, in all situations should be their greatest desire?

Scandalous faith leads a daughter to entrust her life, all of her life to her heavenly Daddy. He is the Giver of Life!!

As we leave the Jairus family are you a little sad too? They feel like family to me, I want to know more. I just have to believe that the daughter, the father, the mother followed Jesus from that point forward. We aren't told but I like to believe they continued to spread the good news of Jesus for the rest of their lives. My imagination prompts me to believe the people of the village knew this little as the daughter of Jairus, but more importantly as the daughter of God.

"Death Was Arrested" – North Point InsideOut

Day Four – Journaling

"Find Me" ~ Johnathan David Helzer, Melissa Helzer

This is your time with God. Journal all that God is impressing on your heart. This page is marked "For Your Eyes Only". If you choose to share your journal it is up to you. There are no little sisters or brothers lurking outside your door waiting for the chance to sneak in and invade your privacy. Go to that place of safety and security with the One who formed you. Be honest with the Searcher of Hearts, oh what blessings await you there!!

Day Four – Journaling

III - HEALING

Step Into The Light

Day One

My Prayer for You ~ Oh God how wonderful You are! I am forever thankful for the words You spoke into the hearts of men thousands of years ago so that today we can read them as though the ink is still fresh on the page. You God love each one of us today just as much as the daughters we are reading about through these pages. Lord, I pray today that You would bend to hear the heart cry of my friend who sits before you with Bible and book open. She is anxiously waiting to hear from YOU! We can't wait to meet You today! We love you, Lord. Amen.

The woman we are befriending this week is one I have heard about all of my life. That may sound strange to some of you, but to know my past you would understand. My experience in church began at six weeks of age. Sunday School, Vacation Bible School and all other things church related were part of my story from the beginning. The leadership in my home church found themselves faithful in teaching the whole Bible. I grew up hearing the stories of more prominent characters in the

Bible. It wasn't, however, until preparing for this study that God began opening my mind and heart to new truths about this woman. For years I had made assumptions about her and her encounter with Jesus. God began to illuminate my understanding of His goodness and mercy through the words of the apostles retelling of this particular miracle. I began to see her as human, not just as an illustration. In her God began to show me a much deeper level of faith than what my mind could conceive. In Jesus I saw a level of love and sweetness that my heart was longing to find. Today I want all of those things for you too. Take the plunge today into the fullness of who Jesus is and who He wants to be for you!

Read Luke 8:42b-48

God actually tells the stories of two daughters within this last section of chapter 8. We have already taken an in depth look at one of the daughters. Now we will complete the chapter by becoming friends with the second.

This daughter is also unnamed, we don't know who her parents are, they aren't mentioned. By the simple fact that she is a woman we know she is a daughter.

In verse 43, how long had the woman been suffering a hemorrhage? _____

In Mark 5:25-26 the same story is recorded, "A woman who had a hemorrhage for twelve years and had endured much at the hands of many physicians, and had spent all that she had and was not helped at all, but rather had grown worse "

Twelve years. I get frustrated if I suffer for 12 minutes. The agony of the suffering she has endured is mind boggling. There are varying opinions of scholars as to the origin of her issue of blood. Some only refer to it as a hemorrhage without giving an origin. While others describe the hemorrhage as an unnatural menstrual cycle. Through the research I have done, I am inclined to believe the latter is true.

Just think about it for a minute, this woman had been on her period for 12 years! 12 YEARS!! The first words that come to my mind are, "Oh bless her heart!!" The book of Leviticus gives very detailed instructions for the people when they are sick or diseased and specifically for women during "their time of the month'.

Read Leviticus 15:19-30

How many days would a woman who was bleeding be unclean according to verse 19?

_____

_____

If someone touched her or anything she had touched, how long would they be considered unclean?

_____

_____

What about the woman whose discharge of blood lasted for many days? How long would she remain unclean?

_____

_____

Wow! Can you imagine? Any other woman would be secluded from the rest of the world from the day she started until 7 days after she finished. That's a lot under normal conditions. During this time she is considered

_____.

As I was studying this woman in preparation for writing, I read over the familiar verses. Early this morning I prayed and asked God to amaze me with new revelation of the stories I've heard since childhood. I begged God to show me something new about Himself and something new about this woman. Imagine with me for a moment what this woman's life must have looked like. We don't really know a lot about her. As I said we don't know her name or her parents. Did she have siblings? Was she married? She had suffered much in those 12 years, not just physically, but most certainly emotionally, mentally and financially.

God often speaks to me through stories, there he brings to life all the details. If you will indulge me, this is how the Lord allowed me to imagine her story. Because I can't bear the thought of her being nameless I have given her a name.

As the sun peeks through the cracks in the window of Batya's room she can hear the rustling of people beginning their day in the town where she lives. Today all she wants to do is pull the cover over her head and dream. Dream... about the way life was before, before she was... well... Then life was beautiful, when she was 12 years old, she was beautiful. Growing up as the only daughter of a wealthy, well respected man in town, she was the apple of his eye. Her father showered her with many gifts. The white linen garments, fit for a princess were among her favorites. To him that's who she was, his princess. Upon returning home in the evenings, her father would scoop up Batya into his arms and twirl her around singing to her a special song. They would dance and sway, twirling and twirling, until with heads spinning they both fell to the ground laughing all the way! She loved Papa and oh how he loved and adored her. Her dreams were filled with all the wonderful days spent cooking with her mother. Mama taught her to bake the bread using just the right amount of oil and flour mixing it all together with love. Everyone in town raved that no other bread tasted as good as her mother's. Batya was learning all she would need to know when she married and started her own family. Her father taught her from the law, the prophets and the writings. She along with her brothers sat at Papa's feet, listening to the teachings passed down from generation to generation. She knew Moses, Abraham, Elijah. Along with her parents and her siblings she remembered the prophecy, expectantly awaiting the promised Messiah. This was a special privilege that wasn't wasted on Batya. She knew that most girls after becoming women had little opportunities to learn the scriptures in such depth. Men studied scripture, women kept the house. Her father treasured his little girl and it was his delight to teach her as well as her brothers.

Batya loved to laugh! Walking to the market was the highlight of her week. She could laugh and talk for hours with her friends. Even as a little girl running through the streets she was full of life. She spent every free moment with her friends dreaming and planning of the day each of them would become betrothed and married. Everyone in the town knew and loved Batya. Her beautiful big brown eyes her dark hair falling in ringlets over her shoulders all paled in comparison to her gentle spirit. But her heart longed to love and care for others.

There were nights she would drift off to sleep wondering to herself about the man who would one day be her husband. Would he be like her Daddy? Would he be strong? Would he treasure her the way her father treasured her mother? One thing she knew, he would study the scripture and he would be devoted to God just as her father was. Oh, yes, she longed to find a man just like her daddy. The time of becoming a woman, even at age twelve was quickly approaching. She didn't fear it. She knew it would come, her mother had prepared her for the day. Once it did, she knew her life would change even if she didn't fully comprehend how much.

She remembered the day as though it were yesterday. Walking with her friends, in the cool of the morning to draw water she was chatting non-stop. She was so excited her friends weren't sure she had taken a breath since she stepped out the front door. Two days ago, her parents introduced her to Saul. He was a good man, no he was a godly man, well studied in all the scripture. Her mother couldn't be more pleased for she had long dreamed of the day her beautiful girl would become a woman and start a family of her own. Yes, she may have been her daddy's girl, his pride and joy, but her mother loved her with the heart of a mama. She knew the desires of a young girl's heart to make a home for her husband, to give him children, to create a life together as a family. Excitedly she giggled with her friends about the plans for the betrothal, which would last at least a year, maybe two. They laughed and talked all the way back home. Batya promised her friends they would spend the next day together baking and preparing for the upcoming festival. Little did she know that afternoon as she stood in the sun waving goodbye to her friends it would be the last time they would make the short trip to the well together.

That night after dinner, as always, the family sat as her father retold the story of Abraham and Isaac. The miracle of the ram caught in the thicket by his horns. Batya thought to herself, "Is there a deeper meaning to this story? How did Isaac feel when he realized God had provided a substitute? Did he remember the sacrifice every time he looked at the herd?" She shook off the questions as her father began the nightly blessing before bed and she joined in repeating the words. Then off to bed she went. Morning broke. She bounced out of bed remembering the day she had planned with her friends. Something wasn't right. She felt different. Something had changed. Suddenly she realized, she wasn't a little girl any longer. Her mother had talked with her many times about this day. She knew what to expect. She knew she would be moving out of her beautiful room with the big windows that allowed the sun to flood in to awaken her each morning. Today she would move to the small room, with only the basic furniture, the small window and the door that would allow food to be passed to her. But it was ok, she knew what must be. And besides it was only for seven days. At the end of those days and after the purification she would no longer be considered unclean.

Abruptly, Batya's eyes flew open as though she had been wakened by an earthquake. For her it was an earthquake, only not physically. That was the last day she had known what life outside the small room built onto the side of each house where the women were separated from the others during their monthly cycle. While this was to protect the rest of the household from becoming unclean for the free spirited Batya is seemed more like a prison sentence. After seven days, then 14 days, then 21 days, then 3 months her family knew something was terribly wrong. Her father spared no expense in seeking care for his little princess. She was seen by every doctor in their town and surrounding villages. Each one with a different diagnosis. Each one with a different treatment. Some of the treatments were easy to administer, others were so horrific even now she must shove them from her memory.

In time her friends moved on with their lives. For a while they would come to the window to ask how she was feeling and bring her news of what was happening in their lives and in the town. Now they hurried past her house or took another route all together. Saul continued to pledge his love and commitment to Batya for two years. But when the opportunity came to study in Jerusalem he sent a letter vowing to always love her, but he couldn't wait any longer. After all this opportunity might never come along again. The stress of caring for a daughter who was constantly ceremonially unclean took a tremendous toll on the entire family. The family had been wealthy when her condition first appeared. But now all the money was gone. Everything had been spent on doctors and cures, none of which made her well and many left her worse than before. Her father as much as he tried, could not shut out the voices and whispers of those in the town who speculated that her malady was a result of sin. Was it her sin? Her parents sin? The rumors at times were vicious. A bitter attack of words and allegations, there was no counter attack on the battlefield of the mind. The attacks grew stronger with every passing year. Eventually, he lost the strength and the will to fight back. The doctors pronounced him dead, the victim of a broken heart. Even now it is difficult to recall the loss of her father only one year ago without bursting into tears. Twelve miserable years Batya struggled with the voices in her head that told her she was dirty every single day. The lies told her that she was responsible for everything her family had suffered. The enemy laughed and taunted that she would always be alone. Who would ever want to marry her or have children with her.

Day after day the fatigue, the loneliness, the shame grew more overwhelming. She had not laughed in so long she wasn't even sure she knew how. Occasionally at night she would venture outside her room. One night when the moon was bright she caught a glimpse of her reflection. She shuddered at the empty eyes who returned her stare. Could that possibly be the young girl who had boldly dreamed of a vibrant future. Where once there appeared a young maiden, now she saw a worn, pale woman. A woman who should have a husband and family by now. How could this happen to her? She felt one hundred years old. Was this some kind of magic? Fatigue overwhelmed her days; the abdominal pain interrupted her sleep. Batya, should have been a beautiful, young woman with glistening eyes, olive skin and white teeth. What was happening? Would she live here in solitude for the rest of her life?

Suddenly, Batya was snatched back into the reality of today. What was going on outside? There was so much excitement in the street outside her window. Just then she heard someone speak the name, Jesus. Yes, she had heard of Jesus. The last time her father had visited her he brought news from the synagogue. This man Jesus was He who claimed to be the promised One, the Messiah.

Jesus healed a man of leprosy. Could it be possible this same Jesus could heal her too. Occasionally she would hear the townspeople on the streets talking about Jesus. From the chair she positioned near the open window she was able to hear the conversations of everyone who passed by. Most revolved around reports of Jesus teaching in Nazareth. A few days before she overheard two men talking about the paralytic who was healed by Jesus words alone. And then there was that centurion's servant. They say he healed him without even being present in the house. What was the story she heard about the woman in Nain? Her son was dead, but Jesus raised him to life. Batya's mind was swirling to the point that she almost became faint. Immediately, a woman began calling out to a friend, "The boat with Jesus aboard is approaching the shore. He has come and we are going with the others to meet him" Batya couldn't believe what she was hearing. Her heart beat faster with each passing second! Jesus is my only hope she thought to herself. I believe he will heal me. Once he hears my story, once he understands my plight he will have mercy on me. I have to get to him. For a moment Batya had forgotten the she was locked away in a prison of law and regulation that would forbid her from approaching the Teacher. How could I possibly approach Him for I am unclean she reasoned with herself. If anyone should see me I will be shunned, ridiculed or worse. What if an old friend recognizes me, will they will run from me? What if Jesus should choose to run from me? Reckless actions of a desperate woman could cause a mob scene. Tears began to well up in her eyes as reality came crashing down all around her. She sank to her knees in despair her head naturally bowed as tears rolled slowly down her cheeks splashing onto the dirt floor beneath her. Slowly at first the words rolled off her tongue, *"My tears are my food, day and night, while all day people ask me, 'Where is your God?' I recall, as my feelings well up within me, how I'd go with the crowd to the house of God, with sounds of joy and praise from the throngs observing the festival. My soul, why are you so downcast? Why are you groaning inside me? Hope in God, since I will praise him again for the salvation that comes from his presence. My God, when I feel so downcast, I remind myself of You..."* Oh God, my God you have heard my prayer, I know where my salvation comes from. My salvation comes from You, O God, maker of heaven and earth. Today, you have heard the cries of Your servant and sent the One who can heal all my diseases. I don't care what it takes I have to try to reach Jesus." In the desperation of the moment she thought to herself, it could work. For so long I have been confined to this room. Batya's frail hands reached for the veil to cover her head and drape across her face. Carefully she grasped the edged to pull them around carefully tucking them so that only her eyes and nose were visible. With head down, watching each step carefully so as not to fall she made her way through the street. At last she was safe inside the crowd. What would all of these people say if they knew who was walking among them? It was a scandalous move, but there was no turning back now. She had opened the door undetected moving into the open space. How she had longed to bask in the sunlight, to breathe in the fresh air of life. All within her hoped that this would be the first of many days spent in the freedom beyond the four walls that surround her for the past twelve years. Cautiously she tried to avoid each one, but the crowd was closing in tighter and tighter. With each person she bumped or brushed past Batya shuddered knowing another unsuspecting person had just been rendered unclean. Silently she asked for God's forgiveness. Batya's heart had remained pure, through the years. When people were cruel, Batya returned kindness.

Suddenly there was a great commotion happening before her eyes? Jairus the synagogue official was kneeling at the feet of Jesus, begging him to come to his house so that he might heal his little daughter. Batya's mind screamed inside her head "This can't be happening. I've taken such a risk! This is my last hope! Jesus, I've waited 12 years, surely you are my only hope. Perhaps it is far too extravagant that I should think to speak to you, it would be forbidden as a woman. I believe, You have the power to heal me. If only I can touch the hem of your garment I know I will be made whole." As she inched closer and closer stretching out her slender arm, reaching her fingers as far as they would go. Biting her lip, willing her body to stretch beyond normal ability. Eyes tightly shut, straining toward the mark, and then…. Yes! There it is!! She felt the fringe brush across her fingers. There her faith met the power of Emmanuel. It was Him, the One, God with us! That's it! Thank you, God!

You my sweet friend cause my heart to burst with gratitude. Thank you, for staying through to the end. I hope as you read the words on paper this woman became more than just a story on a page. My prayer is that God connected with you in reading. These words truly are not my own, but words straight from the heart of God. He had to draw me closer into her story so that I was prepared to receive all He had to teach me as His daughter.

I know today has included a lot of reading. God will certainly bless your faithfulness in leaning in to know Him more. As you finish I would encourage you to sit in the presence of God. His is still our Emmanuel, God with us. He is our healer. Tell Him all that weighs you down today. He wants to hear from YOU!!

"Out of Hiding" ~ Steffany Gretzinger

We All Have Issues

Day Two

One of the things you may have noticed in reading the Bible, some specific accounts of Jesus life and ministry are repeated in the four gospels (Matthew, Mark, Luke and John). Each of the authors may tell the same story from their own perspective. It doesn't mean one is right and the others are wrong. We do the same thing today when a group of people witness an event. Different personalities simply notice different details. We may use different words than others to describe the same event and the same details. Today we are going to look at Mark's account of this same amazing story.

Take a look at **Mark 5:28** to gain more insight to the scandalous faith of this suffering woman.

"For she thought, 'If I touch His garments, I will get well.'" A faith so strong that it would push her past all law, fear, shame, rejection and into His glorious light.

Within this woman and the recording of her story we get an illustration of immense faith. She had been everywhere and tried everything. All her money was gone, spent on doctors and treatment. She was down to her last hope, Jesus. And she was focused on seeking Him.

SEEK. The word is defined as an attempt to find; attempt or desire to obtain or achieve; ask for something from someone. The very word is an action verb. It brings with it the idea of aggressively looking or trying to find something. This woman must have been desperate to find healing. After all, she had spent everything she had in seeking healing. She was now convinced all her time and resources had been spent looking in all the wrong places. On this very day reaching out to the healer was her only choice. For 12 years she had been waiting, watching, begging to count off 7 days. Seven days that never came. Finally, in her heart she believed at the end of the day she would be able to say, "Today is the day!"

The people crowded around Jesus. They had been waiting for Him to return. Someone else had gotten to Him first. The synagogue leader. His daughter was sick. Everyone in the town would have known and loved the little girl. Part of a doting and well-respected family. She was full of life. I wonder if this woman ever looked out the window of her secluded room to see the little girl, Jairus' only daughter, running through the streets, laughing, playing, clean. Think about that word "clean" what images and emotions does that word bring to your mind?

_____

Isaiah 1:18 paints a vivid word picture for "clean", "Though our sins are like scarlet, they shall be white like snow." What are the feelings/emotions you experience when you see fresh snow that covers everything?

Could this really be happening? Before the woman stands Jesus, the one she had longed to encounter the one she had risked everything to see and now He is walking away. Jesus was going to the house of Jairus, a place this woman would not have been allowed to enter. She knew Jesus had the power within Him. She couldn't wait any longer. She had already taken a great risk of being discovered. The crowd was large and she had slipped in unnoticed, but if Jesus left with Jairus who knows how long it would be before He returned. And even if He did return could she slip out unnoticed as easily next time. So, if He couldn't touch her, maybe just maybe she could reach far enough, stretch her fingers out just enough...Yes! There it is just them hem of his robe! Wait! What is that? Can it be true? I know I believed! I know he is the One! I knew He could do it! So, this is what it feels like to be whole, to be free!

How long did it take the bleeding to stop according to verse 44? _____

Wait! What? Can you imagine how that must have felt! If you have ever given birth you are going to understand this example. If you have not yet given birth to a child, you may have heard your mom or another woman speak of this. Think of a woman in labor. The pain is so intense. The contractions can cause every part of a woman's body to ache. Then as soon as that precious bundle is delivered the pain seems to instantly disappear. Years before I gave birth my mother would describe this phenomenon to me. I didn't like pain. I had seen childbirth portrayed in movies and on tv. These women were screaming!! It was obvious they were in tremendous pain. I was convinced it was the worst pain you could possibly experience. Naturally, everything you see on television is the truth, right? Surely my precious mother was glamorizing the truth so that her youngest daughter would someday give her more grandchildren. Obviously, she got her wish. As suspected I experienced excruciating pain, at least until the epidural kicked in to relieve the worst of it. In the moment I vowed I would never forget the pain of childbirth, it would be impossible. There is a reason mother's say these things, because they are true. By the next day, I knew I had pain, but the intensity didn't seem so bad. Oh, and those words I said only the day before. Mama's you know the speech, "I'll never do this again." Yeah, that was history. Some of you may be saying, "You didn't have the same experience I had." I will admit my experiences were not extreme. For those of you who had traumatic labor and delivery experiences, I honor you. In no way would I ever attempt to minimize or make light of what you went through. The euphoria of the hormone overload in almost every case of post child birth will at least for a moment make you forget the pain.

The King James Version sometimes uses words that are not commonly a part of our vocabulary. Some of these words we may have never heard before. There is a connection to one such word within our text for today. I really want you to get the meaning of this particular word and it's best explained with the KJV of verse 44: "Came behind him, and touched the border of his garment: and immediately her issue of blood stanched."

Stanched? This definitely isn't a commonly used word in Alabama. What about you, is the word "stanched" in your vocabulary? We know it has to be similar to "stopped" because that is the word used by most versions of the Bible. The word stanched does mean *to cause or make to stand, to place, to stop, stand still.*

Can you think of any other times throughout Biblical history that God caused something to stop?

Read Exodus 14:13-31.

Just when the children of Israel thought their lives were over or at least their freedom was over, God parted the Red Sea and caused the waters to stand still on either side. The people were able to cross over on dry ground into their new life.

Look at what else God does later in their journey. **Read Joshua 3:7-17**

What did God do to the Jordan River?

_____

_____

Please don't miss this!! Not only did God cause the water to stop flowing. He parted the river, and caused the land to dry so that the Nation of Israel could cross into the land promised to the descendants of Abraham. He also dropped a bomb on the enemy!

Verse 16 says, *"the waters were flowing down from above stood and rose up in one heap, a great distance away at Adam, the city that is beside Zarethan;"*

He caused the Jordan River to back up about 18 miles all the way to a little city called **Adam** so the same people could cross into new life. If you recall, Adam and Eve lived in perfection in the garden where God placed them. There they knew no sickness, no pain, no broken heart and especially no death. Their days were spent walking and talking with God in his holy presence. Until sin entered the world through the first man, Adam. Jesus Christ has the power and the ability to stop the flow of death that is robbing us of life!

The Hebrew word for Jordan means *"descender"*. The root of this word means *to go downward, or to bring down.* Jesus has defeated our "issues", our enemies all the way back to ADAM by overcoming Satan and even death itself in His resurrection. Only Jesus has the power to "take down" our enemy.

"Therefore, since the children share in flesh and blood He Himself likewise also partook of the same, that through death He might render powerless him who had the power of death, that is, the devil." Hebrews 2:14 NASB

Jesus took on flesh so that He could die in our place and free us from the power of our issues. My "issues", your "issues" these are the things that try to drain the LIFE from us. All of these "issues" have no power over us when they are covered by the blood of Jesus. Jesus isn't just a part of my life, He IS my very life!

Reading each of the gospels especially when a certain parable, miracle or teaching of Jesus is recorded is important. It is always dangerous to take one verse out of context. But God can do anything He chooses and He might just choose to bring understanding of a passage to me through the book of Luke. He may want to use the book of Mark or Matthew for someone else. Perhaps John's words speak more clearly to you. As well, today God may speak to me through the New American Standard Version, but tomorrow the wording of the New Living Translation may bring clarity for a specific passage. It is always helpful to read scripture in different versions. We know that "All Scripture is God-breathed and is valuable for teaching the truth, convicting of sin, correcting faults and training in right living; thus, anyone who belongs to God may be fully equipped for every good work." 2 Timothy 3:16-17 CJB

Make the extra effort to read passages from different versions of Holy Scripture because a single word of truth can illuminate a verse to show a lesson never before noticed.

For example, Mark 5:25-26 from the King James Version (emphasis mine) -

> "**And a certain woman, which had an ISSUE of blood twelve years, And had suffered many things of many physicians, and had spent all that she had, and was nothing bettered, but rather grew worse,**"

Issue – wow! The word jumped off the page as I read it this time. Jesus is the only answer to every ISSUE we may ever have. I've got issues, you've got issues, we all have issues. Any time we focus on the issue before us we allow our issue to rid us of the power that God wants for us. We must look to the ONE who is the source of ALL LIFE to be made whole.

The Greek word for issue is *rhusis* which means *a flowing issue.* It comes from a root word which means *to flow.* Leviticus 17:11 "For the life of the flesh is in the blood". This woman's LIFE was flowing right out of her and had been for twelve years! Remember the number twelve in the Bible speaks of government. This condition was governing her life.

Our issues can be overwhelming at times. Even to the point of draining us of our energy and focus. We can try to find the cure through doctors, counselors, drugs, social media, shopping, food, wrong relationships, friends or family. When we are desperate our vision can become blurred. Good sources can appear wrong or bad sources can appear right. But Jesus is the only one who can truly cure us when our life is hemorrhaging out of control. When we humbly come to Him, then and only then can he cure our every issue.

This would be a great time to surrender all your issues to the only one who can stop the hemorrhage and bring life where before there was only sickness and loss. Play the worship song for today and as you listen, write your prayer of surrender to Jesus.

"Tremble" - Mosaic MSC

Found

Day Three

Generally speaking is there anything special about the hem of a garment? The hem of a garment in the first century was quite different than what we imagine today. This hem was special in design and in meaning.

Read Numbers 15:38 – 40 to gain perspective on the design of the garment Jesus was wearing on this day.

What does verse 40 say about the importance of the fringe or tassels?

_____

_____

These would be a holy reminder to the people throughout the generations reminding them to whom they belonged, a holy God. The color blue is significant, it isn't just an easily accessible color of fabric or dye. Throughout the Bible the color is symbolic of deity. It is used extensively throughout the Tabernacle, specifically in and around the Holy of Holies, or the dwelling place of God. Now we find God in flesh, God the Son wearing the very garment that God the Father directed the children of Israel to make for themselves to be worn on their bodies as a daily reminder that they belonged to Him.

Luke retells the events of the day like this, "And a woman who had a hemorrhage for twelve years, and could not be healed by anyone, came up behind Him and touched the fringe of His cloak and immediately her hemorrhage stopped." Vs.43-44.

Being a woman there are just naturally things we do that men just can't seem to comprehend. For instance, what happens when you are out with friends at a restaurant, movie, etc. and you need to visit the ladies room? Do you ask one of your female friends if she also needs to go to the restroom? Why do we as women prefer to go in groups? Another example, sharing clothes. As a mother of three daughters and a female myself this seems almost as a rite of passage. The vast majority of us love to borrow clothing from each other. It was common for my girls to swap clothes, shoes, and accessories with their friends on a regular basis. Men just don't understand our fascination. They don't get into borrowing clothes like we do. I can't think of one time my husband has come home with some piece of clothing that he borrowed from a friend. Now that I think about it though, I would consider it weird if he did! Have you ever wondered why they don't? Maybe that particular thinking within men dates all the way back to Bible times. I'm not stating it as fact, but if it does date that far back this piece of the story might give a little insight.

The fact that the woman touched the fringe of Jesus cloak is extremely significant. This part of the garment of Jesus, the fringe is called the **tzitzit.** The law given to Moses instructed the Israelites to make tassels or fringes on the corner of their garments and to put a blue cord on the fringe at each corner.

This one piece of the verse is far more powerful and significant that anything we could imagine. I truly believe that God put this specific story in the Bible for this specific season of your life. To understand why I would say that we need to do a little more searching into the significance of the garment. When God gives his people instructions for creating something, especially in connection with His house, He always gives very specific and very intentional details. The garment which Jesus was wearing wasn't just an outer covering to keep him warm. He didn't wear it because it was fashionable. Jesus was clothed by His Father. We can trace the intentionality of God's hand throughout the entirety of Jesus life. For our study and to absorb all that God intends to show us as daughters we will focus on the fringe or the tzitzit. We already know that they are important because God gave the instructions for their construction and use. What we may not grasp is the personal importance of the garment to each man. The tzitzit was the most valuable and special part of a man's wardrobe. The only people who were ever allowed to touch the tzitzit were immediate family. If someone other than an immediate family member such as a parent, wife, son or daughter were to ever touch the tzitzit of a man's cloak that single act would be horrifying

Something profound is happening in verse 45-46 of Luke 7. Jesus knowing that His power had left Him asked the question in verse 45, *"Who touched me?"* Can you imagine the look of surprise and shock on the faces of the crowd? They must have been thinking, "Dude, we all touched you. Do you see this crowd?" Even the disciples were surprised at His question. Peter said, there's a huge crowd, everyone is touching you. Although, look at the words in the middle of verse 45 "and while they were all denying it". What could possibly be the reason everyone would deny touching Jesus, although they were crowded around and pressing in to get closer to Him. Just to see Him. Were they after more? How many among the crowd were there in hope of a miracle? If so, why were other healings not recorded? Just a few random questions.

Jesus wouldn't let it go, someone had touched Him and I believe He knew exactly who it was. The woman, who had slipped into the crowd unnoticed, just as she had slipped through 12 years of being unnoticed was about to be seen. She was on the threshold of learning that she had always been seen by the King of Kings.

Why do you think Jesus insisted the woman identify herself publicly?

_____

_____

Read verse 47

> **⁴⁷ When the woman realized she couldn't hide any longer, she came and fell trembling at Jesus' feet. Before the entire crowd she declared, "I was desperate to touch you, Jesus, for I knew if I could just touch even the fringe of your robe I would be healed." TPT**

Have you ever felt like this woman? You thought you had gotten away with something, only to realize the other person knew what had happened? Write down a time when this happened to you.

Is it possible we can all sympathize with this woman? To what degree can you comprehend where her fear may have come from? Could it have been possible she suffered for 12 years because she didn't know Jesus. Perhaps she had heard of Him, but knew He couldn't touch her to heal her because He would then be considered unclean. Matthew, Mark nor Luke recorded interviewing her following the healing. The local news media couldn't interrupt regular programing with a "breaking news" special report including eye witness accounts. That is probably #1,567 on my list of questions I want to ask when I get to heaven. Whatever her reason may have been doesn't matter. What does matter is that she was seeking the One and Only Jesus, the one who would make her clean that day.

It feels pretty safe to say we have all been there at times. At the least we could all probably relate a situation when we were children. My favorite memories of times like these are when the girls were little. Each of the three, at different times, took their turn at cutting their own hair. These are the things which turn a dream into a nightmare for mothers of daughters and sons. I laugh every time I remember the time this happened with Morgan. She was 4 years old the first time she decided that her hair needed a trim. After she cut it and realized I might find the hair she enlisted the help of her big sister, Caitlin. As usual Caitlin had a solution. "Cut your Barbie's hair and put it on top of yours in the trash can. Mom will never know." Now that might sound like it would work. And it might have if not for two problems. One Morgan had brown hair, all her Barbie's were blonde. Two, Morgan didn't have bangs before. Obviously, I noticed the second first and asked her if she cut her hair. She didn't immediately deny changing her hairstyle. But at my persistence she finally told me she didn't. Now Morgan is our third child and what she didn't know yet is that experience is a great teacher. Both of her older sisters had tested their skills with shears years earlier. I got up from the sofa, walked into her room, looked all around even behind the door until…. there it was, hair in the bottom of her trash can. Picking it up I walked back into the family room, held it up and asked, "What is this?" Her eyes grew as big as saucers. There was no denying the brown tresses were once part of her beautiful 4-year-old head. A flood of tears filled the Calhoun home that night, both mine and Morgan's. Today this is just another funny story in the company of thousands of funny stories of our girl's adventures. A memory, an experience, I hope to one day use to console Morgan when her little one cuts their hair the week before Easter pictures.

When we feel, we've done something and gotten away with it a multitude of emotions can course through our system. It couldn't have been any different for this woman. If the people of the town knew she had been unclean, what would their reaction be? If Jesus realized she had touched Him to receive healing how would He react? But Jesus quickly puts all her fears at ease. He calls her out of a twelve-year darkness and into His glorious light.

How does verse 47 describe the way she approaches Jesus?

_____

The woman who had been hidden away for 12 years fell at the feet of Jesus. The majority of the crowd may not have recognized her at first even though they knew her as a child. They looked on as she told her story in front of everyone. Isn't that how it is though? When Jesus heals us, when He changes our story, we tell it, no matter who is in our presence.

Read verse 48.

Jesus responded, **"Beloved daughter, your faith in me has released your healing. You may go with my peace."**

At the end of verse 48 Jesus tells the woman, "your faith has made you well;" It wasn't the act of her touching Jesus that healed her. In Matthew 9:21 we find another account of the same miracle, "for she was saying to herself, 'If I only touch his garment, I will get well.'" She had faith. Her faith was in Jesus, the healer. Her faith in the Son of God motivated her to take action.

There is a Hebrew word for faith, *emunah.* It is a word that means 'to take firm action. This word is less about knowing, more about doing. To have faith is to act. You know a staircase can take you to the next level, but until you climb the stairs you won't experience the next level. She knew healing was available to her through Jesus, but she wouldn't experience it if she didn't take a step of faith. Likewise, we know God loves us and that He knew us before we were ever born. We know He sent Jesus to pay the price for our sin that would allow us to enter into relationship with Him. All of those things are true and lovely. But if we never step out in faith we will never experience the life of a daughter that He so desperately wants to give us.

The Bible doesn't name the woman. We don't know by which name she was known in the village. We aren't even told the name her parents gave her at birth. We do know what the Savior called her that day.

Read Luke 8:48 How did Jesus address her?

_____

"And He said to her, "Daughter, your faith has made you well; go in peace." Luke 8:48

Daughter! When I read that word coming from the mouth of Jesus it makes my heart skip a beat. This is one specific story of another daughter, there are many of us. Yet when we personally allow our hearts to hear it spoken over us by the King of Kings it feels oh so very sweet!

Remember when we were looking at the place of Jesus garment where she touched him. You will recall that this most sacred place on the cloak could only be touched by a member of the man's family. This woman went to Jesus seeking physical healing. But she gained so much more that day. On that eventful day Jesus also welcomed her into His family. He changed her name, her position, her status.

When you were a child, was there a time period when you wish your parents had given you a different name? Maybe as a child you didn't really like your name and wanted to change it to something fancier or something less unique. Were you like my middle daughter Caitlin? My beautiful brown eyed angel went through a time around age 5 when despite my greatest attempts to make her wear hair bows, frilly dresses and to love playing with dolls she wanted to express her own personality. She was obsessed with everything outdoors, rollerblades, bows and arrows and digging in the dirt. I couldn't understand it. I tried to be supportive. But the day she came in and told me to stop calling her Caitlin because her name was "Jason" was crushing all my pink and pretty dreams. This phase lasted for a solid year. Some days I would just give in and play along. There were days I would get upset and try to reason with her explaining how her daddy and I put a lot of thought into the name she was given. It was never anything serious, just one of the many things a parent will walk through during the life of a child. We look back and laugh about it now and lovingly refer to it as "the Jason years". You may, however, remember names that people have called you. They aren't so funny. In fact, they are quite hurtful and can bring you to the point of tears. Words that sound like "unworthy", "unwanted", "loser", "liar", "adulteress", "abortionist", "addict", Those are the names given by someone else, given by a person. The Father wants more than anything to change our name. The names given to us by our society, our enemies, and yes sometimes even our own family members or friends do not tell the story of who we really are. To quote Madea "It ain't about what they call you, it's what you answer to." When I finally stopped fighting Caitlin over what name I did or did not call her and realized that she was and would always be my daughter, that's where peace began. No matter what name she heard me call when dinner was on the table it didn't change who she was on the inside. Her identity was in who she belonged to, not the name by which she was called. The identity of the woman who had suffered for 12 years didn't come from what names she had been called, what she had done, or where she had been. Her identity was found in the One in whom she placed her faith.

What are some "names" you've answered to in the past?

_____

_____

_____

Lay those at the feet of Jesus today and allow him to rename you! He loves you more than you can ever fathom. When the Father looks at you, He doesn't see the things you have done, He doesn't even see the things you haven't done or the mistakes you have desperately hidden from the people around you. He knows you are not identified by any sin of either commission or omission. Those are things you did or things others perceived about you, it is not WHO you are, they are not your identity. Stop now. Don't read any further until you lay down your past. Write a prayer of praise for *whose* you are and *what* He calls you!

_____

_____

_____

_____

_____

_____

_____

_____

"Go in peace" can you imagine being this woman and hearing those words? Peace. She had not known peace for 12 years. And in a moment, the Prince of Peace saw her, He knew her, and He invaded her heart.

Your Father sees you!! Never forget that. When you think He doesn't, remember the words of Isaiah 55:8-9 NLT

> *"My thoughts are nothing like your thoughts," says the Lord.*
>
> *"And my ways are far beyond anything you could imagine.*
>
> *For just as the heavens are higher than the earth,*
>
> *so, my ways are higher than your ways*
>
> *and my thoughts higher than your thoughts."*

Scandalous faith invites a daughter to step out of her comfort zone and into the Light.

How is God calling you to step into the Light?

"Born Again" ~ Cory Asbury

Day Four – Journaling

"I Am Healed"- River Valley Worship

This week has been heavy and eye opening! I am confident God has been speaking to you. What are the issues in your life that God wants to bring to light. Pour it all out in faith to the One who can heal. He's passing your way today. Reach out, He is just a touch away. I'm praying for you and this special time just between you and Jesus!

IV. - FORGIVEN

Chosen One

Day One

The woman we will meet this week is one of my favorites. It may seem strange to you at the introduction of her story that she would be a favorite. If she isn't one of your favorites by the time you reach the end I will be surprised. My heart can easily connect with this one the most. Even though her story occurs earlier in scripture than the others, I chose to explore her story last.

Read Luke 7:36-50

Again, this is another nameless woman. The sub-heading given to this section of scripture in my Bible reads *"Jesus Anointed by a Sinful Woman"*. For centuries, we have been introduced to her not by name, but by her past. How many times has that happened to you? Have you ever been introduced to someone by your occupation? Or maybe even by something you've done in your past? We can even do that to ourselves. Most of our experiences may be more positive than this one. We can often identify with our past mistakes, past hurts or even current occupation. Falling into the trap of identifying ourselves with what we do rather than who we are is common. While Simon and the others may have tried to keep her identity tied to what she did, Jesus definitely sees her as who or more importantly as whose she is.

Simon must have been so proud of himself, hosting Jesus for a dinner party at his house. It wasn't unusual for Jesus to interact with the religious elite. Recorded in the Bible we see Jesus discussing the scriptures with the Pharisees and other leaders. We don't really know all the details around why Simon invited Jesus to dinner on this particular night. There is no mention of the disciples attending the dinner with Jesus or at least they are not mentioned as being seated at the table with him. Traditionally dinner guests would be seated around the table while other people from the town, would gather outside the house to listen in through the doors and windows. Seating at this dinner party would be unlike anything our western minds envision in our extravagant party planning. The invited guests, all men, seated on the floor reclined on their sides with legs curled around so that their feet were behind them.

Read verse 36

"Now one of the Pharisees was requesting Him to dine with him, and He entered the Pharisee's house and reclined *at the table*."

Engage your God-given imagination and creativity as you read these words. The table is set, the men are reclining, people from the town are gathered around outside walls. Just as the party is beginning, a beautiful woman enters the room All conversation ceases as she quietly drifts past each guest. Dressed in the finest garments, her thick dark hair pulled back from her face. The room is pregnant with the scent of a costly fragrance as she moves past the lavishly set table. Quietly, slowly and with intention she passes by the guests who are standing and the other men who are reclining. Her eyes are fixed upon a destination across the room. She is captivated by the object of her destiny, all others in attendance are invisible to her gaze. She is no stranger to the invited guests, everyone in attendance knows her name. The moment she determined within her heart to make the long, lonely walk across town to the home of Simon she settled in her heart the consequences of her actions. There were whispers but her ears only heard silence. As for the others, eyes wide open and searching the room each one in attendance seem to beg the question "Why is she here?" Nervous body language screamed, "Why don't you stop her?" Yet no one moves. Men were covering their faces for fear that she might recognize them thus exposing their shameful deeds. Others one by one, with hand covering mouth gasp at the audacity of the action of this sinful woman. They have all heard the rumors. Many well aware that the rumors are true. The trail of devastation runs deep and wide in this room. She isn't deterred by the shocked glances, gasps or the awkwardness of the situation. Moving through the crowd, past Simon, she is here for one purpose and it isn't to reveal her former client list. At last she comes to a stop and falls to her knees behind the guest of honor. It is as though they are the only two people in the room. The most difficult part of her journey is over. Until this point she had relied on her head to tell her feet to move. Yes, thus far her journey was governed by her head. Her steps were directed toward the One who changes lives forever. She is here, kneeling at His feet. It is now time for her head to surrender control as her heart takes over.

Do you wonder how she was able to enter the house at all? Is it possible she has been to the house of Simon before? Hmm. Perhaps, this dinner was the talk of the town. I'm almost certain everyone knew what was happening that night and who the guest would be. Maybe the entire town was standing outside the walls of Simon's dining room that night. I like to think they were. I like to think everyone in town was a witness to a night they would never forget.

Luke 7:36 "Just as Jesus enters the man's home and takes His place at the table, a woman from the city – **notorious** as a woman of ill repute – follows Him in." (emphasis mine). The Voice Version

Have you ever felt notorious in your hometown? Have you ever had the feeling that everyone knows your sin? Explain what happened and how you felt.

There was a time when I felt like I was wearing a giant flashing sign shouting out all my sins to every passerby. The one thing I didn't want to do was go out in public, especially not to a party. I am positive that I am not the only one who has experienced that feeling. The enemy has had centuries of practice. His craft, temptation, is polished to perfection. He is a master of trickery, enticing unsuspecting victims to see the bright, shiny package never anticipating that we might realize the façade before our eyes. Sin hypnotizes us to believe we are missing the party. Satan's agenda includes convincing us we deserve more, better, or faster. He is good at what he does, I'll admit. But God is so much better. God doesn't have to try so hard to convince us. He never manipulates or threatens us. God is love and so much more. His ways are high above ours, His thoughts are beyond our thoughts. See Isaiah 55:9. Oh yes, sin can seem like fun at first, but the crippling consequences can leave us broken, alone and more disappointed than we were before. Tommy was relaying this illustration to me just last week. Do you remember the movie *The Wizard of Oz*? Dorothy and her friends have heard about the Great and Wonderful Wizard of Oz. By all accounts of the "others" the wizard can give them what they desire. Throughout the movie they have locked their eyes on their destination, Oz. Sure there were roadblocks, warning signs and opportunities to turn back, but the crew forged on toward their goal. Once they finally arrived in the Emerald City, went through everything to get to the wizard something wasn't quite right. Just getting there wasn't enough, the wizard put more and more demands on Dorothy and company, pulling them deeper and deeper into his plot. After the group accomplished all the wizard required of them to receive what they desired the story takes an unexpected turn. The impressive, flashy wizard was bellowing to the motley crew when Toto, Dorothy's dog and constant companion pulls back the satin curtain to reveal a man. Do you remember the words spoken by that man? "Pay no attention to the man behind the curtain." That is exactly how Satan works his schemes. His goal is to make you think participating in sin wrapped up in the package of "fun", "I deserve this" or "everyone else is doing it", is a gift. He works very hard to trick you into looking at the picture and not the man behind the curtain. If he can keep you focused on the sin, then maybe you will never realize he is tempting you. Once he tempts you and you respond then he quickly turns and you are plummeted into a hotbed of shame. If he can keep you imprisoned there he has accomplished his number one goal, paralyzing your belief that God could ever forgive you. Satan can only be successful if you choose to stay there trapped in guilt and shame. God didn't put you there, Satan did. God sent His Only Son to free you from that prison. After being baptized by his cousin John and being tempted by Satan in the wilderness, Jesus returns to Galilee with an anointing of power. He began teaching in the synagogues and was praised. When He came to Nazareth something beautiful happens on the sabbath. The book of the prophet Isaiah was handed to Jesus. He opened it to read. Listen to what He said,

"THE SPIRIT OF THE LORD IS UPON ME, BECAUSE

HE ANNOINTED ME TO PREACH THE GOSPEL TO

THE POOR, HE HAS SENT ME TO PROCLAIM

RELEASE TO THE CAPTIVES, AND RECOVERY OF

SIGHT TO THE BLIND, TO SET FREE THOSE WHO

ARE OPPRESSED, TO PROCLAIM THE FAVORABLE

YEAR OF THE LORD." Luke 4:18-19

Luke tell us in verses 20-21 "And He closed the book, gave it back to the attendant and sat down; and the eyes of all in the synagogue were fixed on Him. And He began to say to them, "Today this Scripture has been fulfilled in your hearing."

Go back up to verses 18-19. Take a pen and above every "He" write in Jesus. Now read aloud those verses replacing "He" with "Jesus". See, it's right there in black and white, Jesus came to set us FREE! Free from the captivity of our sin, you know the one you swore to never tell anyone, the one that causes you to hang your head in shame and avoid the very people who want to love you. Yes, even the sin that others still make a point of reminding you about anytime they are around. Jesus is the One who wants what is good for you. He is not holding out on you, He is holding you!

As you read **Luke 7:37-38** linger over the passage, absorbing every word. There are many details that will seem unusual to our 21st century western culture mind. We will explore those meanings and symbolism later. For now, I want you to absorb the imagery of the environment and the people.

One of the many reasons I enjoy reading the book of Luke is because of the details he provides. In verse 37 we see the woman had something in her hands when she entered the room. As a woman, I find it intriguing that this is the only physical detail we get of this woman. Let's be real ladies, if I knew I was going to meet Jesus I would go to my favorite boutique and pick out the most beautiful dress I could find. Earlier in the day I would have spent hours in the salon getting my hair done, makeup applied and nails painted. The one thing I wouldn't have done was take my perfume bottle with me.

In reality we know nothing of how she was dressed, if her lips were painted or her hair braided with jewels. We only know that in her hands she carried a "beautiful alabaster jar filled with expensive perfume."

Why would these details be so important that they are recorded in Luke's gospel?

Read the following scriptures and record who or what was anointed and what was the purpose?

	Who/what	Purpose
Exodus 29:29	_____	
1 Samuel 16:1;12-13	_____	
1 Kings 19:16	_____	
Isaiah 21:5 ESV	_____	

Throughout the pages of the Bible we learn some specific information regarding anointing with oil. The Hebrew people were very familiar with the practice and requirements pertaining to the anointing of a person. It was a significant event in the consecration of someone or something as holy or sacred. In Exodus we read the requirements given by God in accordance to the anointing of Aaron and his sons as priests. God gave the recipe for the sacred oil to be used in the anointing of everything within the tabernacle, from the tent, the sacred vessels and the priests who serve the Lord. First Samuel records the day in which God chose David as king. We read in 1 Samuel 16 of how Samuel, following the instructions of the Lord, anoints David the youngest son of Jesse as the future King of Israel. David, the one who would be remembered as a man after God's heart. Anointing a king was the equivalent to crowning him. In 1 Kings 19 the Lord tells the prophet Elijah to go find Elisha. Once he locates him the Lord instructed Elijah to anoint Elisha as prophet in his place. In other words, Elisha was chosen by God to become Elijah's successor. In those days the Holy Spirit had not been sent to man. Therefore, the only way men could hear from God was through the prophet. God spoke to His chosen man the message for His people. The man in turn would share that message with the people. There is one other type of person who carried the anointing of God. Isaiah, recalls how the warrior also carried God's anointing into battle. The men are commanded to "oil the shields". The word used for oil here is the Hebrew *mashach.* It is defined as to smear or anoint. By implication it means "to consecrate". In the practical, the shield of a warrior was covered with skin/leather. The oil serves to keep the covering supple and slick. If the outer cover of the shield is slick then the arrows, spears, and other weapons of the enemy from slip past the shield without penetrating it or harming the one behind the shield. Ideally the soldiers would oil their shields on a regular basis. This would prevent the skin covering from drying out or cracking. The faithful of God's army would be led into battle carrying the anointing with them into upon their shields. In consecrating the piece of their armor which can be both defensive and offensive they were declaring to all enemies "The Lord goes before us." The command to oil the shields would be a constant reminder to the weary soldier that the battle was not theirs. The battle belongs to the Lord.

You may be saying to yourself, that's great but what does all of this have to do with Jesus and the woman who entered Simons house with her alabaster jar? Read the following verses to help make the connection.

Hebrews 4:14 Jesus is

_____

Matthew 21:9-11 Jesus is

_____

Matthew 2:2; John 12:12-15: 1 Timothy 6:13-15 Jesus is

_____

_____

Revelation 19:11-16 Jesus is

_____

_____

Oh, my goodness isn't God's Word amazing? It is thrilling to see the beginning of something in the Old Testament and tracing that thing to its fulfillment in Jesus throughout the New Testament. Do you see what a good, creative, unrivaled God we serve? God institutes the anointing of priest, prophet, king and warrior in the Old Testament. Then as only He can do it, we see all of those ultimately fulfilled in Jesus Christ!

I want to pause here for a minute to say, so often I have heard people say they can't read the Bible because it's boring or it isn't relevant today. Confession time, in the past I too have thought parts of the Bible were boring or not relevant to my life. When we connect with God our Father, the legacy of our ancestors will unfold before us. When we fall in love with the word of God only then can the Bible truly come alive as God's love letter to us. Within the pages we find our place in His royal family. Reading God's words to uncover our heritage far exceeds anything our minds can conceive. As a daughter I enjoy finding out about my grandparents, great-grandparents, etc. But I only know their names, birth dates, death dates and possibly place of birth. There are no personal stories that accompany the legal documents I receive from relatives researching our family history. Obviously, I'm not going to have the opportunity to talk with the relatives who have passed from this world. I will never get to read their words or hear them speak to me. If I could, you can bet I would devour every word. Imagine me sitting on the edge of my seat drinking in every story, every lesson and every "I love you"! I'm sure you may have guessed where all this is headed. We have that opportunity every day with God. As a daughter don't we all want to be found sitting at Jesus feet, hearing his words spoken over us, feeling his love surrounding us?

Alabaster was the common substance used for storing perfume or scented oil in that day. The alabaster jar or cruse as it is called in some versions was the best of its kind, and the spikenard was one of the costliest of perfumes. The gift presented by this unnamed woman to Jesus was not something trifle that she had just lying around the house. No, it was a gift worthy of a King. A gift that would be held back for someone she owed a debt of gratitude that could never be paid with any monetary gift. As only he can, Jesus is about to reveal the depth of love which prompted this gift.

We are not told in the scriptures but, I believe this woman knew exactly who was reclining at Simon's table. What if the purpose of God in drawing her was to proclaim another aspect of who Jesus was to the people. Just think about it for a moment. To all who felt small, dirty, insignificant, sinful, unworthy, unwelcomed and unwanted the Father is proclaiming your Priest, Prophet, King and Warrior has arrived! The fulfillment of prophecy was reclining in Simon's house. Salvation for the world was seated at the table of a Pharisee in Capernaum. All invited and uninvited guests alike were straining to catch a glimpse, hear a word, longing for a blessing unaware they were on the brink of receiving more than they bargained for that night. He wasn't here for the elite alone. He was for everyone. The "good" couldn't do enough to earn the right to be with him. The "bad" weren't so bad that they couldn't approach him.

"Extravagant" (Live) – Bethel Music

He Sees Me

Day Two

Have you ever had a conversation with someone when you felt like they were speaking in riddles? I wonder if that is how Simon felt here. Look with me at what has to be one of the most mind-blowing conversations in the Bible.

Read Luke 39-43.

In verse 38 Simon, the host is now a spectator to all that is happening in HIS own home. A woman from the streets has entered his house, crashed his party and captivated his guest's attention. Can you imagine Simon's fury, possible embarrassment and overall disgust with what has transpired? Notice, Simon doesn't voice his feelings aloud. Luke writes, "he said to himself". These words were never spoken out loud by Simon it is merely what Simon is thinking. He said to himself, "IF this man knew what SORT of person this woman is", emphasis mine. The word for "sort" or "kind" comes from a base word which means "dirt" or "soil". In other words, Simon is thinking, if this man, Jesus, was truly a prophet then he should know what sort of dirt she comes from. He is probably thinking this woman is no better than the dirt under my feet. In all honesty, he viewed her as lower than the dirt that clung to our Savior's feet when He entered Simon's house. The same dirt Simon didn't even bother to offer water so it could be washed from his guests' feet. Why did Simon think she was "dirt"? He tells us as he continues his thoughts, "she is a sinner". She isn't just any ordinary sinner, The Greek word used here for sinner is hamartolos, which means "devoted to sin," In no way do I ever want to polish over this woman's past, what she has done, or the relationships in which she had participated. She had been every bit the English word we would give her, harlot. We might call her prostitute or possibly even worse.

There was so much more here that Simon couldn't see through his judgmental lens. Simon saw a harlot. Jesus saw a worshiper. Oh, trust me, harlot was the label of her past. She isn't her past though. Just as you and I are not our past. That past has been ransomed by our Redeemer. She came to Him on this unforgettable night as pure as a virgin bride. She came to thank the One and Only bridegroom. You may be thinking, "Angela, that is impossible. How do I know that?" Stick with me, I want you to uncover the truth for yourself!

God is just so funny!! Oh, to have been alive and outside Simon's house on this night. To be one of the townspeople hanging in the window, listening as the deafening silence was broken by the sweetest voice. Can you imagine the scene? The only sounds in that room for what must have seemed like an eternity were the sobs as she wept and the sound of her lips kissing the beautiful feet that bring good news. Is it possible for you to visualize Simon nervously shifting his weight as he becomes an onlooker at his own dinner party? Does he stare indignantly as this woman poured out her abundant gratitude, love and devotion onto the Master. Though we only get a snippet of what Simon may have been thinking he must have snapped back into reality at the moment Jesus began to speak. The voice of the One who spoke creation into being broke the silence with a request directed at Simon.

Can you see Simon straighten his shoulders as Jesus says to him, "Simon, I have something to say to you?" Picture Simon puffing out his chest thinking, "Finally, here it comes. Woman you are about to get it! It is time for someone to throw this trash out of my house!" Is it possible that for a moment he managed to reel in his pride? For the sake of the other guests he replies, "Say it, Teacher". The great teaching moment was not for Simon alone. This example has endured for all time so that Jesus may teach us as well. We are not only responsible for the words we speak, we are also accountable for the thoughts we think. Jesus demonstrates how he can have a conversation with us even when it seems we are only talking to ourselves. Another reason why it is important to "take every thought captive to the obedience of Christ" 2 Corinthians 10:5.

Simon addresses Jesus as "Teacher" which is very interesting, but it is not the only time we see Jesus given this title. The word for teacher also means "master" or "Rabbi". As Christians, we sometimes think of the Pharisees as being antagonistic toward Jesus. Seeing Simon refer to Jesus as Rabbi could cause a little confusion if we don't understand the relationship from a Jewish perspective. Jesus proceeds to tell Simon the story of a moneylender and two debtors.

Read verse 44

Turning toward the woman, He said to Simon, "Do you see this woman? I entered your house; you gave Me no water for My feet, but she has wet My feet with her tears and wiped them with her hair.

Really take in this scene! Jesus turns toward the woman. Jesus is looking at the woman. But Jesus is talking to Simon. He says to Simon, "Do you **see** this woman?" Simon had been looking at the woman, but he wasn't SEEING her. How many times have you and I looked at someone, but we didn't SEE them? Have you ever felt as though people were looking at you, but they weren't seeing you? Open up your heart to God. You may want to confess times when you have been looking but not seeing someone. Maybe you have petitioned God to allow you to be seen. Know that God does see you. He has always seen you.

When we feel unseen, unheard or unnoticed it can feel overwhelming. This is the place where the enemy can swoop in and attack your mind with accusations. Previously we talked about the warriors who oiled their shields. Ladies, we must be found continually "oiling our shields". How do we do this? We must make prayer, conversation with God our priority. By prioritizing our time spent with God, reading His word, and listening to His voice we will be ready to face the artillery of the enemy.

Jesus saw this notorious woman not only from the moment she entered the room, but her entire life. I believe that Jesus heart broke over her sin and rejoiced over her faith. Could He have smiled when he recognized her bravery in facing those who sought to judge her? Do you think His eyes locked on her as she moved through the crowd? The boldness of her faith leads me to believe she had encountered Him before this day. She knew *this* Jesus, the one who sees beyond the mask, straight into the heart.

Read the words of another woman who understood that God saw her.

"She answered GOD by name, praying to the God who spoke to her, 'You're the God who sees me!' 'Yes! He saw me; and then I saw him!'" Genesis 16:13

Yes, to understand that God sees us is comforting and healing. When we see God then we are transformed.

"Isn't He (This Jesus)" ~ The Belonging Co (Featuring Natalie Grant)

Extravagant Love

Day Three

   The time of learning from three special women of the Bible is quickly coming to an end. I pray that you are listening intently as the Lord longs to speak specifically to you! It has been my prayer from the very beginning that this book/study would not be all about gaining knowledge, but everything about growing into a deeper relationship with God, our Father. My prayer has been that He would shine the spotlight on who He is, the Father he longs to be to you. And in response you will comprehend your identity as a daughter to Him. I pray that the depth and length of His love for you will overwhelm and propel you deeper into the Fathers heart as you pursue your destiny as His daughter.

Compare the things Simon neglected to do with the things the woman did

Simon   **The Woman**

_____

_____

_____

_____

Read Luke 7:47-49

> **"For this reason I say to you, her sins, which are many, have been forgiven, for she loved much; but he who is forgiven little, loves little. Then He said to her, 'Your sins have been forgiven.' Those who were reclining at the table with Him began to say to themselves, 'Who is this man who even forgives sins.'"**

Jesus proclaimed her sins were forgiven. Notice that Jesus never tells her that what she had done in her sin was ok. He didn't make excuses that she didn't have a choice. He never shifted the blame for her actions to her clients or any other outside forces. Her sins were not forgiven because of her actions at the dinner. Two sinners at Simons house that day had the opportunity to have their debts, their sins, forgiven. The woman who was a habitual sinner, the one classified as dirt in the public eye and even as Jesus described her sins were many. She owed a huge debt, one there was seemingly no way she could pay back. The other sinner, Simon judged the woman harshly, he neglected to do the things he knows to do, his sins were more omission than commission. Our human nature sometimes draws us into the trap of classifying some sins as greater than others. All sin is heartbreaking to a holy God. His desire is that his children live in relationship with Him. Sin damages our relationship with Him. If you only look at this story from a purely human point of view, it doesn't take our hearts long to become tender to the woman. To see ourselves as the sinner who has been forgiven much, therefore we love much. I am forever thankful that this story is in the Bible. Many times, I have clung to the forgiveness extended by the Savior. I have fallen on my face, wept tears of both sorrow and joy at the feet of Jesus. Face to the floor, tears soaking my face, with my hair falling across my cheeks. Finally, I am able to rise to my knees. While kneeling I just breathe in and out the clean air and smell the sweetness of the Holy Spirit. It is then I realize the tousled hair now sticking to my cheeks and throat have dried the tears I cried before the Lord. I have laid on my face as one at the foot of His throne and anointed Him with my praise. I have been this woman. I feel like I am her even now. When I close my eyes, this scene comes alive for me, because I shall never forget that I have been forgiven very much!! Therefore, if I fall on my face in adoration of Jesus, if I dance before Him, if I stand and sing with arms stretched to the heavens, if I serve others it is all because I love him so very, very much! He is my song! If I should live 100 years it still wouldn't be long enough to proclaim His love to the world.

Finally, in verse 50 Jesus completes this woman's story in one short sentence, "Your faith has saved you, go in peace."

The Greek word for faith is *pistis* and primarily it means what you would think, "firm persuasion", a conviction based upon hearing. It is always used in the New Testament of "faith in God or Christ, or things spiritual." I know that isn't anything mind shattering. But as I continued researching and reading about the word, God drew my heart closer to Him, to His tenderness, and the idea of how He sees us, He chooses us. He took me to a place of seeing a deeper meaning for this word and how beautifully it relates to this particular woman. When I read it, I knew I had to share it with you. My prayer is that God uses this definition of peace to unlock freedom, forgiveness and joy within you!

I want you to fill in this blank with the particular sin of this woman

_____

Really get this in your mind before God blows it for you. We studied the word. She was a harlot, a prostitute, her sin was sexual. She was no man's wife, she was no man's girlfriend, she was not faithful to any man, before.... Not until she met Jesus. We don't have any record in scripture of when she first believed in Him. We only have a record of the night she exercised her faith in the presence of a judgmental Pharisee and what we can only imagine, a shocked and doubtful crowd. However, I imagine in her mind she was only present in front of One.

Are you ready? Another definition of faith – fidelity! If you're not in tears thank God now that you've never experienced infidelity. And then when you get up off of your knees from thanking Him, get right back down in repentance. We have all been unfaithful to God, the one who truly matters. Until we learn to be faithful to our relationship with God we will always struggle in our faithfulness to others. Our relationship with God is the model for every other one in our lives. When we were born in the flesh we inherited the sin nature of our father Adam. We give our best attempt. We strive for perfection. Even the most religious of Jesus time couldn't keep all the commandments or offer enough sacrifices to remain in a completely faithful state to the God they loved.

Titus 2 explains the faith we are talking about in verse 12. But I want to begin with verse 11.

> **"For the grace of God has appeared, bringing salvation to all men, instructing us to deny ungodliness and worldly desires and to live sensibly, righteously and godly in the present age, looking for the blessed hope and the appearing of the glory of our great God and Savior, Christ Jesus." NASB**

The scandalous faith of this former woman of the street was the thing that compelled her to enter a place where she was uninvited, unwelcomed and unwanted. There she could fall at the feet of the Only One she wanted to see. He alone was worthy of her worship and before a crowd of witnesses she pledged her fidelity.

Hopefully the words Jesus spoke earlier are now ringing in your ears, "For this reason I say to you, her sins which are many, have been forgiven, for she loved much; but he who is forgiven little, loves little." We have all been forgiven a huge debt. Let this be our example to love big, love lavishly!

Take a few minutes to worship Jesus.

Scandalous faith allows us to know we are Chosen by the King of Kings.

"To My Knees" ~ Hillsong Young & Free

Day Four - Journaling

"Reckless Love" ~ Cory Asbury

God has brought us into His family as daughters who are loved and equipped to pour out unrivaled love and devotion. He is the strength we need to stay faithful to our relationship with Him.

Day Four - Journaling

V. - LEGACY

Why Am I Here

Day One

There is a question asked more often than any others. Everyone wants to know "What is my purpose? What am I here for?" Sometimes it comes in the form of a statement but you can hear the question driving "I want to fulfill the destiny God has designed for me." These are great questions, but they aren't as ominous as we try to make them. Jesus spells out the calling for us

> "A new commandment I give to you, that you love one another, even as I have loved you, that you also love one another. By this all men will know that you are My disciples, if you have love for one another." John 13:34-35

> "Jesus answered and said to him, 'If anyone loves Me, he will keep My word; and My Father will love him, and We will come to him and make Our abode with him" John 14:23

"Just as the Father has loved Me, I have also loved you; abide in My love." John 15:9

"And Jesus came up and spoke to them, saying, 'All authority has been given to Me in heaven and on earth. Go therefore and make disciples of all the nation, baptizing them in the name of the Father and the Son and the Holy Spirit, teaching them to observe all that I commanded you; and lo, I am with you always, even to the end of the age.'" Matthew 28:18-20

According to the recorded words of Jesus what do you think about your purpose? What are you here for? How can you fulfill your God ordained destiny?

_____

_____

_____

_____

_____

_____

Jesus told us word for word how to live as daughters of the King. He walked out the example we should follow. He was human in form as we are, he was tempted in the same way yet fully God he showed us the purposeful life God designed for his children.

Satan isn't smart enough to devise a new plan for temptation and honestly why would he when the same ole thing works just fine. His number one goal is to get us to question our faith or our trust in God. Most of the time we make it easy for him to lead us astray. When we listen to his lies we begin to question if God really wants what is best for us. I know, so dumb, but really, we fall for it over and over again. It is as old as time. His words, tactics and methods only change from generation to generation as culture changes. He can glamorize his scheme, change his vocabulary and method from person to person. One thing never changes though, his ultimate goal is the destruction of our relationship with God. To cause us to question God, to question His goodness and His faithfulness. All of this is Satan's desire. He longs to separate daughters from the Father who loves them in hopes they will question everything God says is true.

> "The serpent was the shrewdest of all the wild animals the Lord God had made. One day he asked the woman, "**Did God really say** you must not eat the fruit from any of the trees in the garden?" "Of course we may eat fruit from the trees in the garden," the woman replied. "It's only the fruit from the tree in the middle of the garden that we are not allowed to eat. God said, 'You must not eat it or even touch it; if you do, you will die.'" "You won't die!" the serpent replied to the woman. "God knows that your eyes will be opened as soon as you eat it, and you will be like God, knowing both good and evil." Genesis 3:1-4 NASB, emphasis mine.

There it is! Satan has shrewdly been moving throughout the garden waiting for his moment. He rolls the dice. He takes his shot and blurts out "Did God really say...?" Always remember this is our cue ladies. Take it from our sister Eve any time you hear those words your answer must be a resounding "Yes!! God really did say..." If we read on past Satan or the serpents words we do find that Eve spoke the truth to Satan. She knew what God said, she knew the rules. Unfortunately, I see two mistakes Eve made on that day. First, she added to the words of God. Look at Genesis 2:15-17 "The Lord God placed the man in the Garden of Eden to tend and watch over it. But the Lord God warned him, "You may freely eat the fruit of every tree in the garden—except the tree of the knowledge of good and evil. If you eat its fruit, you are sure to die." Excuse me sister, I don't see anywhere in there that God said, "don't even touch it". Ladies, we must always, always be diligent not to add to the words of God when He speaks to us. We don't want to be found saying "God told me to say this to you...." And then add our own thoughts and words to that.

Now I will cut my sister a little slack, just in case, since we don't have all the story. Maybe Adam didn't trust her? Maybe one day he thought to himself, "This woman God made is like me, but not like me at the same time. I'm over here trying to take care of all these animals, land and still be a great husband. But that Eve, she's got to look at everything, describe in great detail everything. And for heaven's sake WHY does she have to touch everything?" I told you all at the very beginning I have a wild imagination. No, I'm not adding to God's words. I don't understand why Eve added to God's command. Maybe she was an embellisher. Do you happen to know anyone like that? It can be frustrating because you don't actually know where to separate the truth from the embellishment. That is the first place where I see Eve slipping away from the Truth.

Secondly, and actually most importantly, Eve continued the conversation with the serpent for longer than necessary. Once she gave her answer, "Of course we may eat from the trees in the garden, only the tree in the middle of the garden we are not allowed to eat." That should have been the end of the conversation. Move along serpent, I've got better things to do. BYE! But no, she continued talking. Worse, she continued LISTENING to him. When Satan begins talking to you, because he does and he always will, you have one response. SHUT. HIM. DOWN. You tell him your ears are only tuned into the Father's voice. God is your voice of truth!

Satan is counting on you not knowing how the story ends. He's crazy though, God laid it all out for him, the end from the very beginning, "He (the woman's Son) shall bruise you on the head" Genesis 3:15 Jesus the Son delivers the catastrophic blow to end all of Satan's futile attempts to separate the daughters and sons of God from the Father.

We are here to shine a light for all the world to see. We are the daughters of God and we have the greatest mission in all the world, to make His name famous!

"Your lives light up the world. Let others see your light from a distance, for how can you hide a city that stands on a hilltop? And who would light a lamp and then hide it in an obscure place? Instead, it's placed where everyone in the house can benefit from it's light. So don't hide your light! Let it shine brightly before others, so that the commendable things you do will shine as light upon them, and then the will give their praise to your Father in heaven." Matthew 5:14-16TPT

Within the scriptures you have read today and throughout the Bible I believe the reason we are here, the reason God created us and birthed us into His royal bloodline as daughters can be summed up under three main words. Love. Abide. Share. Serve. Because, one I worked for a government contractor for many years who are notorious for their acronyms and two I am always looking for tricks to help me remember names, I refer to this as LASS.

Funny, true story, I am sitting in a coffee shop completing this section. Caitlin is sitting across from me at a table. We have our Americano and Flat White to keep us focused and energized. She's writing and I'm writing. I just begin laughing! Caitlin looks at me with her, "What is it, Mom?" face. And all I can say is, "God!" I had already written the next few sections following this one when I knew I needed to tie them into your reading for today. As I scrolled back to look at the headlines for each day so that I could list them I was thinking of a way to remember them to type the words above. That's when it hit me, love, abide, share, serve. The acronym, LASS. That is when the laughter began. God always goes before us. He knows the beginning from the end. He knows our heart and he knows my heart is to impress on you how deeply He loves you and what a precious, priceless treasure you are to Him. He wrote these words on my heart and in my head long before my fingers touched the keyboard. Lass /las/ *noun* Scottish – a girl or young woman. God, You are so funny! You have loved us from the very beginning!

The song I have selected for today may seem a little different. It doesn't specifically speak to your destiny or God calling you into participating with Him in some ministry. After praying and asking God for a song for this specific section I was listening to a playlist and this is the song that played. It is one of my favorites. If we get right down to it unless we believe who God says He is then nothing else matters. Listen with your heart and believe, because He is _____.

"I Have To Believe" ~ Rita Springer

Love

Day Two

When our girls were small there was a song by Nichole Nordeman "Legacy". During that season of my life I adopted this song as my anthem. The words spoke to the deepest places of my heart and soul. I longed to be the person described in the lyrics. All the girls knew this as "Momma's song". Any time it would come on the radio (yes, it's been that many years) if Claudia, Caitlin or Morgan heard it they would call out "Momma! It's your song." Then they would begin to sing along. Their sweet little voices were as angels to my ears. Their precious faces, their adoring eyes made me want to fulfill what they already saw in me. And as they sang I prayed, "Lord, please let me leave this kind of legacy." The life I longed to live before my children, my husband, my friends and my God.

I wish I could say that I've lived those words every day since then. What I have purposed in my heart is to remember the call on my life to live for Jesus, to love like Jesus and to lead those He entrusts to me to live a life of love.

While I can't tell you specifically if God wants you to be a missionary, preacher, worship leader, mother or teacher, I can with certainty tell you what your purpose is as a daughter. We have a holy mandate to love the Father, the Lord God with all our heart, soul, mind and strength. As a daughter we greet each new day as the greatest opportunity to abide in Christ the Son. What does that mean? Live to be in relationship with Him. Do what you are doing now, get to know Him better. Become a student of the character of God, his great love for you and his Word. Don't just study, put into practice all that God teaches you. There is great truth in the statement "As much as people refuse to believe it, the company you keep does have an impact and influence on your choices." Anonymous. I want to keep company with Jesus. How about you?

We are to love others as we love ourselves. No one ever really wants to mistreat themselves, ignore themselves, hold themselves in unforgiveness or betray themselves. Anyone who would answer "I do" to those questions has a deep hurt that has not been healed. If that is you or someone close to you please reach out to me or a pastor or professional therapist you trust. I want the very best for you. Satan is the one who wants to hold you back in this type of pain. Jesus wants to heal you.

"Legacy" ~ Nichole Nordeman

Abide

"So you must remain in life-union with me, for I remain in life-union with you. For as a branch severed from the vine will not bear fruit, so your life will be fruitless unless you live your life intimately joined to mine." John 15:4 TPT

Life-union equals a lifelong relationship. When we speak of our "destiny" what we really mean is we want to "do something" or "produce" something worthwhile, lasting, pleasing for the kingdom of God. We want to bring glory and honor to Him, to be "fruitful". Jesus gives us the key in this verse. We must abide in Him. That requires something most women struggle with. Being still. Being still doesn't mean being inactive. To be still with the Lord involves listening to His voice, not our own. He is always speaking His instructions and promptings. We must still our thoughts and actions in order to hear Him. It is very hard to hear His voice if we are always following our own desires.

How do we "listen" to Him? We spend time with Him in prayer, reading His word and so important, listening for His voice. I am believing that through our time together you have trained yourself to slow down, stop doing all the talking and really listen for Jesus to speak to your heart.

Real talk here, I love listening for God's voice. It seems I can never predict how He will speak to me. Most of the time He impresses upon my heart His desires, His plans, His love. When I have stilled my heart and my legs I can feel the presence of the Lord. My heart will feel so in tune with His that I am confident that the thoughts I feel impressed on my heart are straight from God's. Many times He will speak to me through a song. It isn't always necessarily through the words of a song, although He does speak to me through those as well. But sometimes a song will trigger a scripture I recall and it speaks to my situation or something God is calling me to do. For this reason it is so important to read His word.

"I am the Good Shepherd. I know my own sheep and my own sheep know me. In the same way, the Father knows me and I know the Father. I put the sheep before myself, sacrificing myself if necessary. You need to know that I have other sheep in addition to those in this pen. I need to gather and bring them, too. They'll also recognize my voice. Then it will be one flock, one Shepherd. This is why the Father loves me: because I freely lay down my life. And so, I am free to take it up again. No one takes it from me. I lay it down of my own free will. I have the right to lay it down; I also have the right to take it up again. I received this authority personally from my Father." John 10:14-18 MSG

As His sheep we do know His voice, we must listen to it, listen to the voice of truth. Any other voice is the wrong one, we must flee from that voice, the voice of a stranger, the voice of a lie.

When God made us daughters to our earthly parents He equipped us with everything we would need to be His daughter. So often we try to overthink and over spiritualize what He desires of us and for us.

Settle within your heart today that you will only fix your eyes on Him. As you inhale His love let it fill your lungs so that every breath you exhale is laden with praise to the only One worthy of praise.

I have shared with you some examples from my life of how I walk out abiding in Jesus. One thing you can be certain of, there are many different ways to abide in Him. Don't get caught up in trying to follow some formula or another person's schedule. The most important thing to remember is that God wants to know YOU!! He wants a relationship with you more than anything. Ask God to let you see Him. He is so anxious to show you. Then follow His instructions. Follow the example Jesus set for us. Most of all follow His heart.

The most important word I would like to give you in discovering your purpose is patience. It makes my heart so happy to see a daughter who is excited about fulfilling her destiny. Far too often I have seen a woman spinning like a top chasing every opportunity that comes by because she wants to "do" so desperately. God isn't looking for our activity, He wants our heart, He longs for our devotion. He might instantly download His perfect plan to you in one day and if He does celebrate. I will celebrate with you. But if this isn't your experience don't despair, God is faithful. He will show you the way. Regardless of when or how you discover God's ultimate plan for your life the most important thing is to enjoy the journey. We get our words so mixed up sometimes. I believe this is a prime example. We say we want to know our "destiny" but what we really have in mind is our "destination". Destiny encompasses everything, every event that happens to a person during their life, including what will happen in the future. Destination is the place to which someone or something is going or being sent. Destiny implies a journey, never ending. Destination is final, it is the place where the journey ends. I don't know about you, but sign me up for the journey, I'll take destiny over destination any day. You can do it!! I believe in you. As you abide in Him, there you will find all the fullness your heart has ever desired HE is always more than enough!

"Endless Alleluia" – Cory Asbury

Share

Day Three

We are to make Jesus known to the world! Our walk as much as our talk should point others to the One who has changed our lives forever. If you knew that the people you meet in the grocery store could see the invisible crown you wear as a daughter of the king, would it change the way you interact with them? What about your family? Are they one hundred percent convinced of your bloodline of royalty? Are your interactions with them evident of love, joy, peace, patience, kindness, goodness, gentleness, patience and self-control? Are you willing to reply in the same way as the prophet Isaiah? When the Lord asked this was Isaiah's reply "Then I heard the voice of the Lord, saying, 'Whom shall I send, and who will go for Us?' Then I said, 'Here am I. Send me!'" Isaiah 6:8. God wants your willingness. He will prepare you, he will provide the way. Give Him your devotion.

Declare as the Psalmist David, "O Lord, open my lips, that my mouth may declare Your praise." Psalm 51:15. God has already given you a story, and there are many who need to hear of the great things God has done in your life. You probably have no idea that within your circle of influence even today someone is held captive in a web of deception or sin similar to what you have already walked through. That dear girl is thinking to herself, I am the only one who has done _____, who believes _____. She needs to know today that she is not alone! She desperately needs someone who has been there but now has escaped by the power of the Holy Spirit. She is longing for someone to reach down a hand to pull her up into freedom and salvation. You have the answer, you know His name. Won't you be the one today? Share the good news of Jesus with your sisters!

"Testimony" – The Belonging Co (featuring Cody Carnes)

Serve

Day Four

You may be thinking, "Wait, day four is journaling." We are deviating a little from our normal week.

Within our legacy as a daughter of the King there is another aspect not always associated with a princess. However, as a daughter of the King of Kings you are no ordinary princess. The crown which sits upon your head is not corruptible. It is not made of gold and gemstones. It is everlasting. Your robe cannot be torn away and given to another. No, the garment you are adorned with is priceless. "I will rejoice greatly in the Lord, my soul will exult in my God; For He has clothed me with garments of salvation, He has wrapped me with a robe of righteousness," Isaiah 61:10. We are all the daughters of God. There is not one crown, one robe, one position. In the royal line of our Father there is room for each and every one of us. Your position in the family of God does not diminish mine, nor does mine nullify yours. God loves each of us and it makes Him so very happy when He sees His daughters encouraging one another in the faith. When one daughter's crown begins to slip the others come along to straighten it, not knock it off her head. Rushing to the side of a hurting sister, loving her and walking with her through a difficult season is one of the greatest gifts we can give one another. You do have a decree to model for the world what this royal life should look like. God has other daughters in the world who will look to you as an example for successfully navigating this life as a daughter of God.

Servanthood was of such supreme importance that Jesus gave this example first to His disciples. His words are recorded and preserved for our benefit today. We can read and understand how highly God esteems serving others.

"For even the Son of Man did not come expecting to be served by everyone, but to serve everyone, and to give his life as the ransom price in exchange for the salvation of many. "Mark **10:45 TPT**

If Jesus, the Savior of the world, believed that serving our friends, family, neighbors and even strangers was important then how could neglect the importance of following His example. You may have heard the statement, "You are never more like Jesus than when you are serving others." There is a great deal of truth in those words. Perhaps you have been part of a church group who serves those in need within your community or church. You may have volunteered at a school, given time with a community group or served others in some way. If so, then you understand the impact of those words. When you are meeting the needs of others something happens within your heart that is unlike any other activity. You come out on the other side feeling more blessed than those you came to serve. It sounds strange but it is so true.

If you are not involved with a group where you have an opportunity to serve others ask a mentor, pastor, leader to help you find an area that is a perfect fit for you and your personality. Check with your church, school and local civic organizations. You will find many opportunities as soon as you begin looking.

Honestly, you don't even have to look that far to find opportunities to serve others. The best place to begin is in your own home. You are probably already doing things which are a service to those you love and share a home with. But where is your heart when you are serving your family, your college roommate, your teammates, your parents, or your husband? To my ladies who are married, let me pose this scenario to you. For years Tommy would get up each morning and iron his own shirt for work before he got into the shower. Recently God began tugging on my heart that I should iron his clothes for him. I mean I already knew this but I was stubborn. Understand, Tommy did not expect me to iron his clothes, in fact he would always say that he liked or maybe he didn't mind ironing them. This had nothing to do with who did or did not do the ironing, or expectations within our marriage. It had everything to do with my heart. At first, I would get up and iron, no joy, no love, no song. Just obligation to fulfill a promise to God. God began working on my heart each time I ran that hot iron over the white cotton shirts. As the steam rose around my face and the smell of fabric softener filled the room I sensed the Holy Spirit whispering to me, "This is a perfect time to pray for your husband." He was right. As I began to thank God for the gift Tommy is to our family my heart toward ironing softened. When I prayed for protection over Tommy's health I remembered all the times he had been strong when I was weak. Tears began to fill my eyes as I remembered the prayers my own Mama had prayed for the man I would some day marry and realizing God had created Tommy perfectly just for me. I smiled as I thought about the wisdom God has given Tommy, his work ethic and discipline in learning all he can in his career. Discipline and integrity of character has placed him in a position where God has blessed him with the ability to provide for all the needs of our family. I'm not sure exactly when it happened, but sometime within that conversation God allowed me to see that I wasn't just performing a menial task, I was serving my husband. That day changed my life. Even on occasion when I am tempted to get frustrated, feel unappreciated or I am just tired, I remember it isn't about me. It's all about Jesus. I GET to serve my family. I GET to serve my friends. I GET to serve my community! It is all because of Jesus and for His glory. He changed my heart that day and honestly, I pray I am never the same again.

> "Whatever you do, do your work heartily, as for the Lord rather than for men, knowing that from the Lord you will receive the reward of the inheritance. It is the Lord Christ whom you serve."
>
> Colossians 3:23-24NASB.

Can you think of a way God may be calling you to serve? What about the people or areas you have never thought of before. I believe you are far more powerful, more talented, have a greater depth of wisdom than you have even begun to imagine. God is longing for you to see yourself as He sees you. You are worthy. You are capable. And you have a heavenly Father who is cheering you on.

Why don't you pour out your heart to him in prayer below? You might just be surprised at all God shows you.

"For The One" – Bethel Music, Jenn Johnson

A Few Final Truths About Daughters

A daughter will laugh with you until your sides split, she will cause you to cry buckets of tears, both happy and sad. She will ditch you for her friends but come running to you when her heart is broken.

A daughter is the jewel in your crown.

Regardless of who your earthly parents were, their parenting style, whether you felt loved, wanted or treasured by them or not. You have a heavenly Father who is crazy about you!! Just listen to what God says about YOU!

"Behold, children are a heritage from the Lord, the fruit of the womb, a reward." Psalm 127:3 ESV

"Do not fear, for I am with you; I will bring your offspring from the east, and gather you from the west. I will say to the north, 'Give them up!' And to the south, 'Do not hold them back.' Bring My sons from afar and My daughters from the ends of the earth, everyone who is called by My name and whom I have created, even whom I have made." Isaiah 43:5-7. Though God originally said these words over Israel, we are all descendants of Abraham. He wants to gather all of his daughters (and sons) to Himself.

You aren't an accident. You may have heard those words spoken over you, but listen to me today, that is a lie! You are a gift from our heavenly Father to the world. He told you that in Psalm 139. You are His glorious masterpiece, signed by the artist, Elohim, God our Creator. We are his works of art. His signature on your life is what makes you special. It isn't what you look like, it isn't what you do. It is all because of whose you are. You are a gift. You are beautiful, you are smart, you are enough and you are a treasure because of the sacrifice of Jesus. You are made in the image of Christ. And because of His sacrifice you are made worthy!

Today, I would like to encourage you to listen to Sons and Daughters by North Point InsideOut as we conclude our time together. Thank you, God, for choosing us! As the words of this song surround you and fill the atmosphere, worship the God of Heaven who knows your name. It is Daughter!

Bask in His presence as you worship the Father.

"Sons and Daughters" ~ North Point InsideOut

10 Things About Being God's Daughter

1. **He wants to teach me to feel every day how deeply He loves me.** Through the story of Jairus God demonstrates that He is a good father. We learned through the study of Luke 8:41-56, there is no limit to His love, there is no limit to the length in which God would go to bring a daughter into relationship with Him. There is no limit to my love for each of my girls. I don't want them to just hear me say "I love you". I want them to feel it deeply, all the way to their bones.

2. **He wants to hear about me, from me, not from someone else.** Again, He taught this truth in Luke 8. Anyone could have told Jesus about the woman with the issue of blood. He could have just gone on his way with Jairus. But I believe Jesus wanted to hear about her life, her story from her. The same is true for my girls, I don't want to hear about their lives from someone else. From the moment I became a mom of girls my mission was to cultivate a relationship of open honesty. I've always wanted them to feel comfortable and confident in telling me about their lives, their success and their failures. Nothing hurt me more

when the girls were younger than hearing some great news about one of them from someone else. Especially from another mom of one of their friends. Through communication and focusing more time on strengthening our relationship as mother/daughter, spending more time together just talking about life in general we formed relationships that each of us longed for. The same is true with our Heavenly Father. It is what He longs for and I know it is what you long for as a daughter of the King. It's how you were created. He wants to hear the good and the bad from YOU!! Tell Him!

3. **He wants me to stand confidently in the fact that I am unique and it is frustrating to try to force a different personality upon myself.** I might admire certain traits in another person. Yes, I set a goal to be more organized, more creative, to speak without a southern drawl. But here is the one thing I do know Psalm 139:13 promises me, "For You formed my inward parts; You wove me in my mother's womb. I will give thanks to you for I am fearfully and wonderfully made; Wonderful are your works. And my soul knows it very well." God made me. He made me the way He wants me. Yes, He teaches me, leads me, and encourages me to grow every day to become more like Him. So, I will strive to be more organized, more creative, and more disciplined. I will thank Him that He chose the Southeastern United States as my birthplace. He will continue to work on me to embrace my southern drawl and I will trust Him in the process. God created each one of us uniquely. There isn't another one exactly like you. Good news, God

doesn't compare you to another one of His children. He has a unique love for each and every daughter. You cannot be replaced in His heart. Because you are a unique creation, He has a unique love for you. I don't want to take your place in the Father's heart and I don't want anyone else to take my place. Isn't that in essence what we are saying when we envy how God has made someone else. When we compare ourselves to another sister we are in a way saying to God, "I don't think you got it right for me." When I read those words in black and white I am shocked. The audacity of my heart to imply that I might know better than God what I should be is horrifying! Our position in God's family and our place in His heart cannot be replaced with anyone else. I don't know about you but I'm perfectly content with the unique way that God loves me.

4. **You can run, but eventually you run back home.** In Luke 15:11-32 Jesus tells a story about a prodigal child to all those who were gathered to listen. Although scripture is telling the story of a son, it is equally applicable to daughters. Many times I have chosen my own direction. Trying to do life my way without seeking my Father's wisdom I was setting myself up for disaster. How many times have I ended up in an emotional, financial, spiritual pig pen. Eventually coming to my senses I ran back to my Father, just like the son. Praying He would take me back as a daughter I turned toward home. If my rebellion was too much to forgive I prayed He would at least allow me to serve Him. Have you felt this way too? All my heart desired was to be in His presence. I want to be fed the Bread of Life though His words. Did you ever try to run away from home as a kid? Please hear my

heart here, I am in no way or would I ever make light of a real runaway. My heart aches for any of you who have ever experienced the anguish as a mother who spends countless sleepless nights in agony over a child that you can't wrap your arms around. What about the mother who doesn't know where her beloved daughter or son is living. I weep for you sweet daughter who felt that running away from your situation was the only option you had. I pray that you found healing, restoration and acceptance. Some of us from great homes romanticized the idea of being on our own away from home. As a young girl I sought momentary independence. I was about six years old the day I decided to pack a bag and run away to greener pastures. I got as far as the back steps. Sitting on the steps for the next 30 minutes contemplating my next move, I saw my Daddy's car pull into the driveway. He was home from work! I leapt off the steps, ran to his door just has he got out of the car, and jumped into his arms! He was home! I was home! And I never wanted to leave again!! Sometimes it takes putting distance between us and home for our hearts to focus on what really makes home, "home."

5. **Sometimes you just need to be, you only need to crawl up in momma's lap.** There were times throughout the years until the day my momma passed away that nothing made sense. I couldn't fix things. All I could do was "just be". The only thing that made me feel better was if I could crawl up in momma's lap and let her rock me. After I became an adult many times I would sit beside her and lay my head in her lap. As she stroked my hair

an unexplainable peace would flood over me. There are still days where I long to be able to do that, just one more time. The same is true with our heavenly Father. When things seem to be going crazy I close my eyes and imagine myself safe in the arms of God. As He strokes my hair all the tension, confusion and doubt slip away. I am experiencing a peace that passes all understanding because my Papa, my Abba is in control.

6. **You can never escape momma's love, you are never too old to need the love of a momma.** Can you remember when you were around 15 or 16 and all you could think about was growing up, becoming an adult, when you wouldn't need anyone else. You could do it all by yourself! I can't think of a sadder world than one where mommas don't exist. That's the kind of love that chases you down, smooths over the scrapes and scratches and reminds you that regardless of how old you are, you will always be her baby. There's nothing you can do to stop her from loving you. God loves us like this. Nothing can ever take his love away from us. He tells us so, "And I am convinced that **nothing can** ever **separate** us from God's love. Neither death nor life, neither angels nor demons, neither our fears for today nor our worries about tomorrow—not even the powers of hell **can separate** us from God's love." Romans 8:38 NLT

7. **A daughter can bring the deepest pain and the greatest joy all in a matter of minutes.** She has the potential to take your heart on a rollercoaster ride. It isn't anything intentional, but when her

heart breaks, your heart breaks. When she is elated, you are elated. When she succeeds, you celebrate right along with her. When she suffers a failure, you pull out all the stops to encourage her and help her to pick herself up and try again. As daughters of God we are His greatest joy, but oh how His heart must break when we turn from Him.

8. **A daughter is an instant first love, an endless love.** I will never forget the moment I laid eyes on my first born, Claudia. I had never felt such overwhelming love for anything in my life. That day I knew in my heart I would never feel that again, nothing could ever consume so much of my heart, ever. And nothing or no one did, until June 3, 1992 when Claudia's little sister, Caitlin was born. An unfathomable miracle was occurring in my heart as I was consumed with love for Caitlin, yet the love I felt for Claudia was diminished. It seemed unreal. Then it happened again on July 9, 1995 when baby sister, Morgan was born and the cycle began all over again. How could it be that the human heart could feel total love for more than one person. God loves us instantly and forever. When one more daughter is added the love He has for you or for me is not divided, it is not diminished, there is always abundant love for each one.

9. **You can tell them something 100 times, but they won't get it until it's time for them to get it.**

10. One day, even though they swore it would never happen, a daughter will finally say, "I'm turning into my momma". Admit it ladies, we've all said it. And maybe there are character traits, quirks of our momma's that we genuinely hoped we wouldn't inherit. There are just as many good qualities of my momma that I see in myself every day. One of my favorites, every time I look down at my hands I smile because I see her hands. My knuckles have the same creases as hers did. My nail beds are shaped like hers. During the summer, I see the same olive skin. But what I hope my children see are the hands that lovingly caress their cheeks. I hope they remember my hands, as I remember Momma's carefully turning the pages of the Bible that she loved so dearly and faithfully read. I pray that God blesses me someday with grandchildren and that they will remember my hands lovingly working in the kitchen preparing a meal for my family. The more the years pass I embrace the truth that I am turning into my mother. But more importantly I want to say I'm turning into my Father's daughter. "Dear friends, we are already God's children, but **he** has not yet shown us what we will be like when Christ appears. But we do know that we will be like **him**, for we will **see him as he** really **is**." 1 John 3:2.

Mothers let me encourage you here. You can endure the sass, the eye rolling, the messy room because you know...one day she will be the mother. Lead them well while they are in your care. Trust the Father as he instructs and leads you. Remember the words of Philippians 4:8-9MSG. Summing it all up, friends, I'd say you'll do best by filling your minds and meditating on things true, noble, reputable, authentic, compelling, gracious—the best, not the worst; the beautiful, not the ugly; things to praise, not things to curse. Put into practice what you learned from me, what you heard and saw and realized. Do that, and God, who makes everything work together, will work you into his most excellent harmonies.

NOTES

NOTES

NOTES

ABOUT THE AUTHOR

Angela Calhoun is a girl in love with Jesus Christ and the word of God. Her passion is to see people grow in relationship and knowledge of God as they understand their identity in Him. She has been a Bible study leader, small groups pastor and continues to lead women in pursing their God appointed destiny. She is a daughter, mother, wife and sister. Angela and her husband Tommy have three adult daughters, Claudia, Caitlin and Morgan.

Made in the USA
Columbia, SC
03 July 2018